Medicine, Justice and the Bubblegum Factory

A Memoir

Graham Standen

The Book Guild Ltd

First published in Great Britain in 2019 by
The Book Guild Ltd
9 Priory Business Park
Wistow Road, Kibworth
Leicestershire, LE8 0RX
Freephone: 0800 999 2982
www.bookguild.co.uk
Email: info@bookguild.co.uk
Twitter: @bookguild

Typeset in Garamond

Printed and bound in Great Britain by CPI Group (UK) Ltd, Croydon, CR0 4YY

ISBN 978 1912575 794

British Library Cataloguing in Publication Data.
A catalogue record for this book is available from the British Library.

Medicine, Justice
and the
Bubblegum Factory

To my wife and parents.

Contents

To my knowledge, all the events described in this memoir are true, but in some instances names, and occasionally genders and locations, have been changed in the interests of patient confidentiality and personal privacy.

Preface

Promiscuous rock stars documenting their cocaine-fuelled decline, poor little rich girls sharing the benefits of spells in rehab, and sad celebrities trapped in dysfunctional lives of fame, wealth and emptiness. Or personal battles with obsessive hoarding, kleptomania or the compulsion to feed slot machines. The memoir can be many things. However, you have come to the wrong place if you are expecting such a story. This is a gentle tale of a working-class lad from Romford making his way in the world. A turbulent childhood in the '50s disrupted by a father's absence at war, maternal illness, a short spell in a children's home and fostering with relatives before receiving his final badge of underachievement: eleven-plus failure; followed by a child's view of life at a secondary modern school in the '60s, coming of age at university in the '70s and my experiences working as a hospital doctor and leukaemia specialist in the '80s. Some whimsy, nostalgia and the occasional poignant aside — and not forgetting a subplot describing the premature deaths of my father and his two brothers from an occupational cancer and our family's battle for justice, a story of corporate neglect and indifference which provides insight into just how far major companies will go in the pursuit of profit. You will be no wiser about the preoccupations of celebrities at the end of this memoir, but I'm fairly sure that, should you choose to share my journey, you will not return home empty-handed.

Although I am the narrator of this story, and use the thread of my life from birth to middle age as a framework, the tale is primarily about my parents; their lives, love, last days and legacy. My wife is also a key character in the play as she quietly influences the unfolding story. So you might note references to virtues which have become less fashionable of late, like moral principles, integrity, loyalty, trust and self-sacrifice. Ancient words which sometimes seem to have become anachronistic in the modern world.

Having lived the life described in this memoir and written the words that comprise it, it is difficult for me to read it with fresh eyes and give an objective view of its tone or message. But I hope that it is an uplifting tale. Pain and sadness are part of the human condition and can rarely be avoided. However, the spirit of the age of my childhood and early adulthood was generally optimistic for most people, most of the time, and I hope I have captured that positive note.

Virtually all the individuals I describe have passed a test. In some way, large or small, directly or obliquely, they have had a positive impact on my life and contributed to the person I am today. Whether relatives long dead, lifelong friends or passing ships in the night, I am grateful to them all for their gifts. At the end you might conclude that I have been very lucky, and I would not dissent from that view. Whether people make their own luck or not is one of the grand paradoxes of life and perhaps this memoir will help you decide. In any event, I hope you enjoy it.

1

Sweet Smells of Bubblegum and Tilbury Marsh

The strong, sweet smell of flavouring concentrate drifted from the ball-rolling drums, stinging the eyes and catching my throat. I might have passed comment if I could have raised my voice above the thunderous clatter. The air was full of dust, and it was nearing the time for food dyes to be added before the final ladle of boiling syrup. In the future, industrial health and safety inspectors might have turned apoplectic. But in the A&BC bubblegum factory in Romford in the early 1970s, it was all in a day's work for Terry, Charlie, Brian, Fred (the gaffer) and his son, Gary.

I had sought holiday employment at factories in a light industrial estate on the edge of town and was pleased that my second phone call was successful. Apart from the heat, dust, noise and thick, aromatic odours, the work was physically demanding – tipping large, heavy trays of grey, unprocessed bubblegum balls into drums like cement mixers and later removing the shiny, bright pebbles after all the additions. But I was young, energetic and eager to earn the cash. Could it be any worse than my previous job lifting baked loaves from a conveyer belt for twelve hours through the night at the local Co-op bakery? An activity which left me with a lifelong aversion to the smell of freshly baked bread.

The small team was a close-knit group. Terry would not have looked out of place in a modern-day boy band. Good-looking and trim, he had a nimble mind and was curious about my life and ambitions. Charlie, a gruff family man, had a thin black moustache and a hint of frontal balding which gave him an appearance of premature middle age. Over time, the jagged edges of his personality softened and he became kinder as we worked together in the harsh conditions and our friendship grew. With a blond quiff and a delinquent swagger, Brian carried a trace of menace which was subdued by the camaraderie of the group. Like goading a rattlesnake with a stick, four of us would periodically leap on him and wrestle him to the ground in the dust; legs and arms flailing in mock battle as he cursed and eventually succumbed to the weight of numbers. The leader, Fred, sat like a toad with a pot belly and exophthalmic eyes in front of a boiling cauldron of syrup, and his only role seemed to be adding the final ladle of scalding liquid to the drums at the end of the process. Spare and urchin-like, with a black fringe and pallid skin, Gary completed the quintet and was the Artful Dodger to his father's Bill Sykes.

As it happens, a two-month stint of manual labour in this tough environment provided insights and skills which would be invaluable in my future career. Learning how to get on with people from all walks of life was a priceless asset to have in my toolbox. I was not from a well-off or entitled background, but I was a student – which in those distant days came with automatic social baggage. Only a small percentage of the population went to university and it offered a plausible possibility of social advancement. I knew, consciously or not, that if I came across with any educated airs or graces in this workplace I would not last long. As a postman's son with five years at a secondary modern school behind me, it was not difficult to remain down to earth and become one of the lads. It also did no harm that they could see that I was not work-shy and, bit by bit, I became accepted by the group. It was just as well that I made the effort since, as the end of my summer vacation approached, Terry matter-of-factly informed me that, on hearing a student was joining them, they had all been determined to make my life difficult and my stay at the A&BC factory short. On the last weekend, as a final act of male bonding we all made our way to a local park and watched Terry play football, and I left them with sadness, knowing that our lives were taking different paths which were unlikely to cross again. A few years later, the bubblegum factory burnt to the ground and persisting memories are all that now remain of that time.

For those who don't know its people well, Romford has acquired a rather unsavoury reputation of late. It has a long history, however, as an Essex market town with strong associations with the brewing industry. As a boy, I remember being given a tour of the Ind Coope brewery with my best friend, Billy Higgins, and his father, who was a gateman at the plant. Like the baking bread, the dense aroma of hops has stayed with me, though with perhaps less antipathy.

The population of Romford was swollen in the 1930s and '40s by an exodus of the poor from London's East End. Set in rural South Essex as it was then, the boundaries expanded with the post-war housing boom and London families were able to breathe clean air and make a fresh start in the new suburbia. Hitherto, brief experiences of the countryside were, for many, limited to trips to the Kent hop fields where primitive accommodation, hard labour and a small payment passed for an annual holiday.

My parents were part of this outward migration. Betty was born in Bethnal Green within the sound of Bow Bells, and my father, George, lived in Canning Town. They had difficult lives punctuated by tragedy, and their story provides a valuable perspective of working-class life in the middle of the last century. Betty together with her seven brothers and two sisters were orphaned when she was eight years of age. With her baby sister Dorothy, she was taken in by Mr and Mrs Ayres who lived next door and were childless.

The children were never formally adopted, but it would seem that the couple were caring and loving as stand-in parents. After moving with the two young girls to Marlborough Road in Romford, both Mr and Mrs Ayres died and Betty, by then in her late teens, took on the role of Dorothy's guardian. Leaving school when she was fourteen, my mother started work at the local Pioneer Laundry, promptly becoming infected with scabies from the dirty washing. Later she would travel, Monday to Friday through the war years, to Petticoat Lane in the East End, where she worked as a machinist in the rag trade. By this time my father was in the Royal Marines, signing up as a regular in 1939 after previously working with his father and two brothers on the construction of power stations along the Thames Estuary. The story goes that Betty's sister, Rene, struck up a conversation on a train with George's mother, Alice, who, in characteristically generous fashion, invited her to a forthcoming family party. Rene couldn't make it, but persuaded my mother to go – and George, in Royal Marine uniform and with Hollywood looks, answered the door. A coincidence which would begin all the unfolding events of my life.

Many of my paternal grandfather's (John Senior) wider family worked on the docks along the Thames. Grandmother Alice was one of nine children, but records show that five had died before 1911. The family lived in a tenement block in Silvertown and, together with her mother and several sisters, worked in the Bryant and May match factory in Bow. Schoolchildren will know from their history books that white phosphorous was used in the manufacture of matches in the latter half of the nineteenth century and many workers suffered poisonous effects from it. In particular, the chemical caused 'phossy jaw', an occupational disease characterised by abscesses and eventual destruction of the bones of the jaw. My ancestors would have avoided such misfortune by just a few years as the less toxic but more expensive red phosphorous superseded the white. The matchgirls' strike of 1888 was a key event in the history of organised labour in Britain, when the female workers at the factory successfully fought against child labour, unfair grievance procedures and poor pay as well as the serious health risks of working with white phosphorous. Fighting exploitation by callous factory owners, the strike was generally recognised as an inspiration for the development of trade unions throughout the country in the twentieth century.

After they were married, and shortly before I was born in 1949, George and Betty, together with Dorothy, set up home in a small ground-floor flat in Manor Road, Romford. With my father often abroad with the Marines, life was not easy for my mother. In fact, life would never be easy for my mother. There was a firstborn, my brother Stephen, who died of gastroenteritis. Tales of deprivation were quite usual for the times, with a tin bath in the kitchen, an outside lavatory and hiding from the tallyman before payday on a Friday. With George away, Dorothy repaid her debt of care to my mother by helping to look after me as an infant; a close brother-sister relationship developed, which probably accounts for our enduring bond.

To describe a first memory has become a discredited narrative device in memoirs on the grounds of cliché. In my case, however, the earliest pictures in my mind carry rather more significance than most. At the age of two and a half I spent a month in Ardmore Children's Home in Buckhurst Hill on the edge of Epping Forest. My mother had brought a small gift with her from the overcrowded and insanitary living conditions of the East End, namely, pulmonary tuberculosis. At that time, this disease was a frightening scourge which had little in the way of effective treatment and was commonly fatal. The Ardmore was originally used as a refuge for wartime single mothers, but was later requisitioned by the Department of Health to isolate the young children of parents with tuberculosis to minimise the risk of cross-infection before they received the BCG vaccination. The vaccine was first used in 1921 and was given safely to thousands of children over the following decade. However, confidence in the approach must have been severely damaged in 1930 when 250 infants in Lübeck, Northern Germany were given a preparation contaminated with a pathogenic strain of mycobacterium, which resulted in 208 becoming infected and seventy-three deaths. Perhaps this tragic episode was still in the collective memory of the authorities when they advised that we be segregated away from the security of our families. I remember standing as a toddler in a cot in a shared nursery, and the garden of the home with gladioli in bloom. Feelings of abandonment and bewilderment must have sharply imprinted the images in my young mind.

My father left the Royal Marines in 1953. I recall standing with my mother on the quayside in Chatham as my father arrived on the cruiser HMS *Belfast* from Korea. At least, I think I remember because we have a small vinyl recording disc, made at a booth on the quay, containing a recording of my mother prompting me to voice my greetings, and perhaps this has replaced a true memory of the event. What I definitely remember, however, is accompanying my father on board, leaning back whilst sitting on a form in the mess room and lacerating my scalp on some cast-iron metal casing. Later, my mother would use the visible scar on the back of my skull as a marker for an effective short back and sides whenever I visited a barber! More recently, I unsuccessfully sought out the fitment responsible on a tour of the ship, which is now a museum moored by Tower Bridge. The tour nevertheless shone a brighter light on my father's wartime experiences, which were otherwise only glimpsed via half-remembered conversations and a few blurred photographs.

In the same year we moved to a council house in Jutsums Lane, Romford, and the quality of our living conditions improved. A brother and sister arrived, but during this time my mother continued to suffer chronic ill health from the tuberculosis. Having left the services, my father gained employment as a postman. This was a not-unusual path for unskilled men leaving the military – the hierarchy, uniform and camaraderie providing a familiar bridge to Civvy Street. However, the inevitable progression of my mother's illness reached a critical point and she endured a number of primitive surgical procedures at the London Chest Hospital to 'rest' the damaged lung. Air was syringed into the pleural cavity to collapse the infected organ and, later, ribs were excised to reduce lung expansion. Despite the ineffectiveness of this disfiguring surgery, my mother spoke of the surgeon, Mr Vernon Thompson, in hushed tones of awe, respect and gratitude. Fortunately, she avoided the most bizarre surgery available at that time: so-called plombage, in which numerous table-tennis-size plastic spheres were inserted into the pleural cavity to prevent the diseased lung expanding. Modern-day medical students would surely be mystified by an X-ray from this era showing a chest full of ping-pong balls.

Eventually, Betty was advised to enter a sanatorium located in rural Essex with the rather darkly prophetic name of Black Notley. In the absence of any effective treatment, fresh air and adequate nutrition was the order of the day. To be fair, given that the disease was associated with poverty, poor living conditions and malnutrition, this was not entirely fanciful. However, the regime was harsh, with patients wheeled onto verandas in the depths of winter where snow collected on the counterpane. This was not the worst experience for my mother, however. She had a lifelong phobia of birds, and she described her terror as they hopped along the foot of her bed.

For the family to survive, my father needed to work, and simultaneously caring for three children was out of the question. There was little option other than for we three to be fostered. By this time I was around eight years of age and well established in Crowlands Primary School. It was agreed, however, that I would go to live with my Aunt Lal and Uncle Arthur in Grays; a town close to the Thames Estuary in South Essex. Never an attractive location, the area was perhaps less deprived, run-down and blighted in the '50s than after the deindustrialisation of later years, and the even bleaker descriptions of more recent social surveys. There was an ancient pub in nearby Tilbury called the World's End, and nobody would argue. My younger brother initially lived with Nanny Alice, but would later follow me to Grays. My sister, on the other hand, was fostered with a couple in Brentwood.

Lal and Arthur were kind and their three children, all older than me, seemed to accept the cuckoo in their nest with few complaints. The eldest, David, would tell me many years later that I was quite miserable, but I do not remember it like that. A rare photo from the time shows me in short trousers with an impish grin and a jauntily cocked schoolboy cap. The pose and garb would not have been out of place in London's East End in the 1930s, and indeed, we have just such a picture of my mother's brother, Charlie.

Given the separation from family and the unfamiliar environment, it has always surprised me that I do not have more unpleasant memories of this period. As with the children's home, however, I do have some very sharp recollections of life in Grays. There was the time I sat with long-forgotten school friends in a quiet side road in still summer heat, idly popping the heads off hedgerow flowers. The road led to a factory manufacturing ice lollies, and we often chanced requests for free treats, which were occasionally successful. Although my aunt and uncle were good parents in loco parentis, my cousins and I were given greater freedom to wander and explore than I was used to at home. We roamed through wasteland towards the river and the desolate squalor of Grays beach, examining rusty oil drums and other river debris, but avoiding the occasional rotting animal carcass in the long grass. Sweet smells from local factories would sometimes catch on the breeze; the Bata Shoe Company the most likely source across Tilbury Marshes to the east. I watched cargo ships trudge up the river towards the wharfs and quays of the Port of London, where my father's family worked on the docks fifty years before.

The sense of smell provided another evocative reminder of the time. We made a short trip along the estuary to holiday on

Canvey Island. In 1953, before the large housing developments of later decades, this area suffered serious flooding with major loss of life. Five years after the event, the wooden chalet still had an all-pervading, musty smell of the salt marsh. We bathed in muddy creeks, and in my mind's eye I can see banks of *Crustacea* shells washed up by the swollen tidal waters. There was great excitement on our return as we left the railway station and were met by two black-and-white taxis – a Vauxhall Cresta and Velox. I had rarely, if ever, travelled in a car before.

Black inkwells with scratchy pen nibs, hundreds and thousands from the sweet shop, and *Davy Crockett, King of the Wild Frontier* at the cinema. I have memories of wandering through allotments with a curly-haired girl of similar age and returning to her home at teatime for a sandwich of chocolate spread. During another early evening of long shadows and fading light, I ran with my cousin, Jean, in and out of the buildings of Tilbury Fort as my aunt and uncle sipped tea in the cafe. Small craft bobbed in the gullies and a ferry gave plaintive blasts on its horn as it plied its way towards Gravesend.

It must have been an enormous challenge for my father to continue working whilst spending his free time visiting the family displaced around the four corners of the county. Occasionally, batches of letters would arrive from my school friends in Romford, which were gratefully received. However, I do not recall any intense feelings of homesickness. Equally, when I returned home after just less than a year, I do not remember any great sense of elation. Perhaps this tells us more about the resilience of children in general than my exceptional bravado or strength of character.

My mother had been fortunate. A number of highly effective drugs active against tuberculosis had been developed in the late 1940s (streptomycin, para-aminosalicylic acid and isoniazid), and the newly established NHS meant that she could afford to be treated with these agents. The therapy lasted nine months and I remember her taking the flying-saucer-shaped sachets with every meal. We returned to our former life in Jutsums Lane and my period apart in Grays became what it has remained to this day; a dreamlike interlude.

Although I was registered to attend the local school in Grays, the disruption inevitably impacted on my education. Soon, the day came to sit the eleven-plus examination – the once-in-a-lifetime opportunity to be accepted into a grammar school with the promise of superior teaching, better educational facilities and status in the eyes of friends and family. There would be the anticipation of social advancement, assured personal growth, a useful network of well-placed friends in the future – and, of course, wealth. There might even be the opportunity to progress to university; a rare achievement for a working-class lad in those days. In the '60s, if you went to grammar school there were no excuses for complaining about life chances.

I failed the exam abysmally. I vaguely remember a request to identify the name of a rodent from the anagram *tra* and writing *art*. Only two children from my class of thirty were successful, so it would probably have made little difference if I had smelt a *rat*. Before the penny dropped, I could not understand why so few in my class had passed, and yet virtually the whole year at a school in the wealthier Collier Row succeeded in reaching their nirvana.

There followed an odd period of uncertainty as I chose a secondary modern school to attend. St Edward's Church of England School was closest and had the best reputation as an educational institution, but we were not a religious family. My father was nominally Church of England but had never attended for worship. In fact, when Stephen died, he was heard to say, "That's it, I'm an atheist – there is no God." My mother, with the maiden name of Daltrey and originating from the East End, was descended from Protestant Huguenots fleeing Catholic persecution in France in the early eighteenth century. Paradoxically, she leaned towards Catholicism when she was young and, in fact, my siblings and I underwent Catholic baptism. However, both my parents lost any residual faith in later years – presumably because of the barrage of tragedy, family misfortune and poor health they had endured in their younger lives.

The Warren School in Chadwell Heath was also a single bus ride away, and was the destination of most of my friends. This choice was duly made and the completed forms sent to the Education Department. Except that it wasn't! At the last minute, and for some obscure reason, I changed my mind and decided to attend Pettits Lane School on the other side of town. True, my mother had attended the school in the 1930s but I don't remember this having a significant influence on my change of heart. We managed to reverse the bureaucratic cogs in the Education Department and fate took another hand in guiding my progress through life.

Albert's body had already begun to cool as the heat drained from the day in the late-August afternoon. He lay still in the corner of a twenty-four-bed Nightingale Ward in Harold Wood Hospital; his features in death little changed from the waxy mask worn in the last few days of his life. Only an hour before, I had gently attempted to pass some water between his dry lips, and now his body no longer needed sustenance of any kind. I was employed for the summer vacation as a ward orderly, but in the late 1960s there were no carefully worded job descriptions. I doubled as a nursing auxiliary and essentially I could undertake most activities on the ward short of distributing medication.

I shared ward orderly duties with Harry, one of the permanent hospital staff. He was a Jack-the-Lad in his fifties, diminutive with bottle-bottom glasses and a brisk line of patter. His cheery good humour was a useful commodity on the geriatric ward where he was popular with the old men, sharing repartee and innuendo. He also had that priceless knack – indeed, some would say gift – for appearing to do much while in fact doing very little.

"I'll just pop over to the kitchens to check the menus for the week," he would say as I set to cleaning the lavatories, wiping the bottoms of old men and changing pyjamas splattered with various excretions and secretions. Or, "I need to have a word with young Nurse Swinton on Ward C; we are thinking about working out some new social events for the old boys." He wouldn't be seen for an hour and his grand initiative would never be seen at all. Harry was certainly going to take advantage of a student's energy and industry while I was there, but the really annoying thing was that, as a character, he was so difficult to dislike.

The qualified nurse on duty was Cathy, fortyish, dark, squat and giving every appearance of being hard as nails on the outside and having an even tougher core on the inside. It would not have surprised me if she had had a military background. Curiously, however, the geriatric ward of old soldiers and sailors, who had all fought in at least one of the World Wars, responded well to the gruff but ultimately kind care she dispensed. I have sharp recollections of the elderly men who resided on the ward during my ten-week stint. Many had had strokes and were immobile – in their dependency, so grateful for any kindness – or were in the advanced stages of dementia and required patience and compassion. Often only the hollowed-out shells of their personalities survived, but echoes of their characters were glimpsed in individual foibles and repetitive phrases, uttered in thin, cracked voices. Having lived long lives, they commonly radiated a calm acceptance of their fate. There were also occasional flashes of wisdom; Charlie imploring me to enjoy my life as "forty years pass in the blink of an eye".

Following Albert's death, Cathy took me through my first 'laying-out' procedure: gently washing the body, plugging the orifices, supporting the sagging jaw and dressing the corpse in a thin white shroud. The arms were placed across the chest, and replacing Albert's false teeth would make him more presentable when relatives came to view the body later. I gave him a last look before I closed the curtains, washed my hands and went to prepare the evening drinks.

It has become a truism that recent generations have had significantly less exposure to premature death and dying than those in past years. Some have explained the morbid grief which followed the death of Princess Diana as a manifestation of this phenomenon. Death commonly punctuated with full stops the years of my childhood and adolescence. I was born shortly after the end of the war, and loss and bereavement continued to permeate the thoughts and conversations of our family and community. My mother and father had many siblings, and both my mother's half-brother, Charlie Tunstall, and my father's brother, John Standen, perished in November 1941 when the light cruiser HMS *Dunedin* was sunk by a U-boat off the coast of Brazil. In fact, it was this common bond of family bereavement which encouraged the conversation in that train carriage between Nanny Alice and Auntie Rene that led to my parents' fortunate union. I have previously mentioned how the tragedy of Stephen's death must have continued to resonate with my parents, probably until the end of their lives. George's sister, Eva, died at an early age from a gynaecological malignancy, leaving two young sons, and cancer continued to whittle down the numbers of my uncles over successive decades.

My cousin was six when he died of acute lymphoblastic leukaemia, a tragedy made all the more poignant by the fact that this disease can now be cured in 90% of affected children. As if this was not enough to bear, the Divine Powers decided that his father, Richard, should succumb to the industrial disease mesothelioma in his mid forties. Although some compensation was forthcoming, his widow was left with four young boys to bring up alone. A classmate in primary school died in a tragic accident and I still remember his face and, unnervingly, his character from sixty years ago. The out-of-step student with a bow tie, sports jacket and Wooster-like air who committed suicide in the first week at university, and the depressed workmate whose professional career had prematurely slowed – and was then brought to an abrupt close. These events were tragic for everyone involved, but the list is not meant to be a morbid catalogue of grief. It shows, if anything, that death is an inevitable part of life's text and that perhaps recent generations have had less opportunity to deal with the psychological consequences of the full stops in the treatise. Or perhaps for some, a question mark would be more appropriate punctuation.

Late last year, my wife and I were enjoying a trip to China which was high up on our bucket list. In Beijing the sky was sunny and cloudless, but there was something not quite right. The city was bathed in an electric-blue haze and, like the atmosphere in the bubblegum factory, the air caught in the throat and stung the eyes.

The high levels of pollution in Beijing took my mind back to the early 1950s and my childhood in Romford. Known as a pea-souper, a thick yellow-green smog was common in London at that time and was composed of soot and the poisonous gas sulphur dioxide. I remember walking with my mother in streets which were virtually unnavigable because of poor visibility, and we took shallow breaths through scarves held close to the mouth. Back home, my mother would cough and hack. For someone with damaged and infected lungs, the chemical soup of dirty air must have caused serious harm. The most lethal episode occurred in 1952 and resulted in the Clean Air Acts of 1956 and 1968. These were to have a major impact on public health, but it was many decades before access to clean air became a right in the private as well as the public domain. In the 1950s and 1960s smoking was widespread and was embraced by the large majority of friends and family. To travel on the upper deck of the bus to school was to enter a dense fug of tobacco smoke which lingered on the hair and clothes for the remainder of the day. A visit to the school staffroom was also a far from pleasant experience, and many of the teachers must have felt more than a hint of hypocrisy as they instructed us on the hazards of smoking. It would be 2007 before the smoking ban was introduced to the UK. Personally, I found the behaviour of smokers odd; like pigeons trained to press a button for the reward of a morsel of pleasure. In my young mind, I had performed a risk assessment and cost-benefit analysis and decided against the idea. And in any event, it seemed more rebellious in those days to be a non-smoker. My contrarian nature fortunately helped me avoid the smoking epidemic, but the lives of many others of my generation were blighted.

About 350 million Chinese smoke and there are nearly one million deaths each year, mainly men. It will be interesting to see how an authoritarian government manages this menace to health. Smoking and atmospheric pollution are not their only public health concerns, however. On our trip I was convinced that the sterilising effect of contamination with heavy metals and other pollutants was the only reason that the pathogenic protozoa cryptosporidium and giardia failed to flourish in the tap water. All the hard-won battles for public and occupational health that we fought in the last century are still to be overcome by China in this millennium.

2

Flagship of the Eastern Fleet

During our trip to China, my wife fell into conversation with a recently retired brigadier as we sailed on a cruise boat along the Yangtze River. He looked the part: tall and handsome, with a military bearing but an easy charm which allowed him to interact comfortably with the different demographics and social strata of our tour party. Somehow, they got onto the topic of fighting men, the challenges of command, managing their psychology and bonding in groups during the intensity of battle. Also, how ordinary men can be transformed into killing machines. My wife related some of the wartime experiences of my father as a commando in the Royal Marines. She could not resist telling the story from my childhood of when George, on a rare occasion, described the assortment of weapons he was familiar with, including the Bren gun, the Lee-Enfield rifle and the Sten machine gun.

"And what was your favourite weapon, Dad?" we small boys asked.

"Oh, a cheese wire, I think," came the reply.

The brigadier gave a loud, hearty laugh – he recognised a fellow old soldier.

This story may be apocryphal and Dad was probably playing

to the gallery. However, it summed up neatly how war changes the perspective of good men when family, friend and country are in peril.

Like many returning servicemen, George was reticent about describing his experiences in the Second World War and he did not generally glorify its brutality. What little information we have suggests he saw heavy action on the light cruiser *HMS Liverpool* supporting convoys attempting to reach Malta which was besieged in the early phase of the war. And my mother said that he occasionally hinted at painful memories of hard battles and close combat in the Italian campaigns of 1943. Later, photographs of my father in uniform or football gear allow his progress east to be followed as he is pictured in Singapore and eventually Hong Kong. A handwritten note appears beneath a picture of the *Belfast* in Kure, Japan. The ship's service record reveals that it was detailed to collect the first wave of Allied prisoners of war from detention camps in the defeated country. On a tourist trail to nearby Hiroshima not long ago, it was a curious feeling to look across the inland sea to where my father stood all those years ago. The *Belfast*'s records for the Korean War document close cooperation with the US 7th Fleet as the ships bombarded various targets on the east coast of the country. This was not without an enemy response, however, as the lists of fatalities and casualties of the ship's company show. Other comments give small insights into life on board as the *Belfast* plied between Hong Kong and ports in Japan and Korea.

Feb. 23rd 1951: Operations on W. Coast, Korea. Temperature on deck 9°F [–13°C].
Nov.18th 1951: Sailed for E. Coast. Bombardment of Hŭngnam with rocket ships.
Dec. 23rd 1951: Xmas in Hong Kong. What a party!
Feb. 6th 1952: Fired 56-gun salute for H.M.'s [George VI's] death.

It is difficult to imagine how these Technicolor experiences of naval life might have impacted on this simple man from the East End with hitherto limited horizons and opportunities. He had a special respect for the Indian and Gurkha regiments he fought alongside, and no doubt the regard was mutual. I never heard him utter a word of prejudice against anyone, whether based on colour, caste or creed. He surely thought that when you need someone to cover your back on the battlefield, you look rather deeper into a man than the colour of his skin. As fate would have it, in a future hour of greatest need, an Indian workmate who revered my father would step up and remain by his side.

There was no doubt that George was a brave man of principle and integrity. He was the first to step forward when ordnance broke free in severe weather in the South China Sea and volunteers were required to secure it. The flagship of the Eastern Fleet pitched and rolled as the full force of Typhoon Ruth threatened to overwhelm the cruiser. The *Belfast*'s records describe the six-inch shells *rumbling and clanking* below decks, and he was commended for helping secure the munitions. It was also no surprise that, on a later day trip to Southend, he jumped fully clothed from a jetty to save a young girl who had slipped into the currents. No one offered assistance and he spent the remainder of the day and the train journey home to Romford in sopping clothes.

I have already described how he worked to keep the family together in times of great adversity. Apart from his hand-rolled tobacco, which was of brutal coarseness and pungency, he had no vices and was a loyal, faithful husband and loving father. Nevertheless, in many ways George was an absent parent during our childhood. As he was abroad during my first three years, my mother and aunt were largely responsible for my early upbringing. Later, after he joined the Post Office, we could only make ends meet if he worked night shifts and punishing hours of overtime. On one winter's evening, he set off for work and fell off his bicycle after falling asleep. For some reason, at the time, I found this to be hilarious, but the sadness of the story and my thoughtless response later filled me with shame.

He had a typical cockney sense of humour and I can remember the belly laugh that he shared with his mother and I occasionally find myself echoing; an audible mannerism cascading as a trait through the generations. He could also be gently chiding. When I foolishly described the large waves I had encountered while bodyboarding in Cornwall, the man who had ploughed through typhoons in the southern oceans replied, "What, as high as this house, son?"

Yet he could also be eccentric. Because we had no car, and household rubbish was difficult to dispose of, George would periodically dig an enormous hole in the back garden and fill it with the family's debris. Such precious finds for metal detectorists in the future!

We were never without a pet dog, and Peter was a cross collie idolised by the family but untrained and having no hint of self-control. My father decided that, to save walking the dog, he would attach him by a long chain to a line that ran the full length of the garden. This was not a bad idea – until Peter broke free. On the first occasion, he tore round to Green Stores, the local grocer's. On entering the shop with the loose chain flailing behind, total carnage ensued. It was many months before any member of the family could enter the shop again. After a similar episode in which Peter laid waste to the ripening produce of a friend's father's allotment, it was time to abort the experiment. The family as a whole had succumbed to contrition fatigue. In his declining years, Peter broke a back leg and the family descended into a pit of despair. Eventually, the decision was made for the vet to pin the fractured limb at a cost of £200 – which very likely bankrupted my parents for the next six months.

So what else can I tell you about my father which may surprise you? Well, he could knit and perform expert embroidery. I remember this quiet man of action fashioning a beautifully embroidered fire screen bearing an image of a galleon in full sail;

a picture which would later recur in different circumstances. There was a long tradition of such crafts amongst sailors in the nineteenth and early twentieth centuries as they passed the long hours in port or in open sea. Dexterity with needle and thread was already established to darn sails, repair clothing and sometimes embellish tunics with fine needlework. Delicate embroideries composed of different-coloured wool yarns were known as 'woolies', and often showed portraits of the sailors' vessels. It has been speculated that their inspiration came from the Chinese embroideries sold to naval men in Hong Kong and the treaty ports.

This gentle counterpoint showed a different side to my father and, along with his integrity as a working man and dutiful breadwinner, George's character was never in doubt. He was a great role model for a young boy. He was also very good-looking, with more than a passing resemblance to Errol Flynn – and I have yet to forgive him for not being more generous with those genes!

The London Borough of Havering Heritage booklet of 1998 records that Jutsums Lane (as Judson's Lane) was shown on an Ordnance Survey map of Essex in 1871. It strikes me as odd now that the single row of council houses on our side of the road was adrift in a sea of owner-occupier dwellings. Perhaps it resulted from a paternalistic planning department attempting to engineer a mix of different social groups, or the housing needs of staff in adjacent public utilities. A station was planned where the Great Eastern Line crossed the road further down, but this was shelved in the 1930s. In any event, the houses, though relatively substantial, stood apart in their bland frontage and the choice of paint given by the council; either chocolate brown or institutional green.

The social geography of the area in my childhood is best described by taking an imaginary journey from Romford Station in the centre of town towards London's Liverpool Street. In the mile to the bridge over our road, the chimneys of the Ind Coope brewery would be the first encountered. From my visit with Billy Higgins

I had inside knowledge of the drying rooms, fermentation tanks, conveyer belts and barrel stacks hidden behind the anonymous walls. And then the gasworks, a complex maze of pipes, grey metal hardware, escaping steam and brooding gasometers. The virtual absence of humanity recalled a Charles Sheeler photograph of solitude on an industrial scale. Further on was Romford Greyhound Racing Stadium, now an anachronism as one of only two tracks remaining in London. Perhaps its fortunes could be restored by reintroducing cheetah racing after the abortive attempt in 1937. The enterprising entrepreneur failed to recognise that, unlike dogs, cats of whatever background cannot be persuaded to overexert themselves unless there is an obvious reward. After Jutsums Lane, the vista would soften with the green spaces of St Edward's School playing fields and West Ham United's training ground coming into view.

The neighbours on one side were a large, salt-of-the-earth family who were nevertheless decent and we got on well. They were even less well-off than we were, and on one occasion my parents took their youngest with us on a cheap week's holiday to St Osyth on the Essex coast. On the other side were a retired railwayman and his wife. I considered them very old, but they were probably prematurely aged by hard lives and heavy work. He generously gave us toys from a different era and also a collection of 'tobacco silks', rectangles of satin material of various sizes colourfully printed with flags, footballers, Chinese ceramic artefacts or famous paintings. They were included in packets of cigarettes or cigars early in the twentieth century and were designed to be collected in sets or quilted together. Produced in their thousands, they are worth very little but I have kept them as a memento of another time.

We often received knocks on our chocolate-brown front door from tradesmen. The Co-op baker and milkman would ask for the 'divi', or dividend number, a forerunner of supermarket loyalty points. This number – 231611 – was written on the door frame by my mother but she needn't have bothered – I remember it to this day. On a Friday morning the lemonade man would call for payment, and once a month, John Taylor would appear. Our clothes were all bought at his small outfitter's in Goodmayes, no doubt because he was happy to offer tick. We would visit every six months and the payment could be staggered in between. Wearing a camel-hair coat and with a cigarette between his fingers, he was a hybrid of two actors from different eras; the coarse facial features and physique of Edward G. Robinson combined with the Estuary whine and throaty glottal stops of Ray Winstone.

It would be wrong for me to overstate the strictures of poverty. My mother took pride in having us well turned out, and my father's navy habits ensured that we all had clean shoes and were scrubbed and tidy for school and visits to Nanny Alice. We were never hungry. Basic food was always on the table and Mum's pastry, although relatively high on the Mohs' scale, was always eaten voraciously by her young family. And there was always a joint for Sunday lunch, but never chicken – it was too expensive and, as you will remember, my mother had a phobia of birds. Pork pies were also rigidly excluded from the menu. The assertion that Mrs Ayres died after eating one was never questioned and we were all tutored to avoid the risk of fatal food poisoning by this foul means. The crusty savoury carried mortal threat and never darkened the door of Jutsums Lane. Aunt Dorothy, who was five years of age at the time, recently questioned whether, in fact, Mrs Ayres felt queasy and left a pub after eating a meat pie, only to be hit by a passing car. A twist that would have furnished an unexpectedly humorous climax to the story – albeit in poor taste. However, my wife's skills in exploring newspaper archives and death certificates disproved this alternative history and the morbid veil of suspicion continues to hang over this delicacy in our family.

When George had left for his night shift at the Post Office, my mother initiated a well-rehearsed regime. She had always been an anxious woman and, in the absence of my father, had an unnatural fear of intruders. We would retire early to one bedroom where my mother would sleep in her double bed with my younger brother and sister, one to each side. I slept in the corner of the room on a camp-bed-cum-put-you-up. This arrangement was not necessitated by a lack of space – the council house had three bedrooms. In Mum's mind, being in one compact location provided security, should there be any unexpected threat in the night. The hall light remained on and Peter, our dog, took up his familiar sleeping position on the landing and acted as sentry.

Having described the scene with a slightly condescending tone, I have to say that this unusual arrangement did give a rare opportunity for the family to engage in idle gossip and anecdotes, and discuss any notable events of the past day. Often these would be light-hearted – perhaps speculating on how we might spend £75,000 if we won the football pools. On other occasions, my mother would describe life and friendships in the sanatorium or recount her experiences in the war. Her concerns for the ten-year-old Dorothy when, at the beginning of the Blitz and with anti-aircraft artillery posted at the end of Marlborough Road, she was evacuated to safety with family friends in Devon. She travelled alone and was met at the destination by a couple she had never met. How my mother hid beneath her seat on the Liverpool Street train as it was strafed by German warplanes and bullets rattled on the roof. Or how, on leaving her Anderson bomb shelter in the morning and surveying the street, a large, smouldering space had appeared where a house previously stood. The sadness she felt for old neighbours who perished in the Bethnal Green Tube Station disaster in March 1943, when panic induced by an impending air raid led to 173 people being crushed to death. She described the different forms of fear induced by the V1 and V2 rockets directed towards London in the last months of the war. In the case of the former, one would wait with bated breath for the engine to cut out before the inevitable explosion and random destruction. The speedier V2, on the other hand, struck terror with no warning.

With these stories as part of her history, it would be insensitive for anyone to consider my mother's proneness to anxiety as a character flaw. All these events can be corroborated by independent eyewitnesses and I'm sure she sanitised some of the stories for our young ears. For example, an air-raid warden's diary reported that the house destroyed in Marlborough Road resulted in the deaths of thirteen people including eleven children. What is so notable now is that she was describing events which had happened just fifteen years or so before.

"I'm Brian; let's have a good time!" cried the figure garbed in pillar-box red at the front of the large dining room, his false jollity only just hidden by his beaming smile. Descriptions of poorer families in the '50s and '60s often include a first visit to a Butlins holiday camp.

Billy Butlin's innovative idea of affordable, communal fun in refashioned army camps by the sea has become a staple of popular comedy over the years. The first camp was opened in 1936 and the chain offered a splash of colour in the otherwise drab routine of working-class life, particularly before the cultural revolution of the Swinging Sixties. Poor accommodation in wooden huts with basic sanitation, mass catering and military-style regimentation were gladly accepted in return for the unfamiliar experiences of nightly variety shows, ballrooms with mirrorballs, swimming pools with glass walls, and endless days of organised sports and afternoon bingo. We went for several holidays at the Clacton camp as I turned ten years old, and I'm not ashamed to say that I had a brilliant time. Dad was also in his element, taking part in the athletics, football and tug-o'-war. It was great to see him enjoying himself and catching up on his sleep for once. We were reminded of his true character – the fun, humour and generous nature.

Both my mother and father had what in modern parlance is called an authoritative style of parenting. We knew what behaviour was expected of us and the penalties if the rules were broken. One day at the camp I pestered my mother for a tiny penknife, and eventually she grudgingly acquiesced. Her misgivings must have increased as I began acting silly and throwing the knife into the grass verge as we walked back to the chalet. Inevitably, I lost the knife, and despite both of us searching the square foot of ground for an age, it never surfaced. I think I had reached adulthood before it dawned on me that my mother must have quickly spotted the knife and quietly confiscated it. On this occasion she cleverly achieved her objective with minimum fuss *and* inflicted a penalty for my foolishness in one furtive manoeuvre.

Pettits Lane School was situated in a well-to-do area of Romford, but the social mix of the pupils was diverse and one suspected that most children of families in the immediate vicinity were destined to go to local grammar schools or more distant private schools. The building was symmetrical with two separate halves for girls and boys. Girls were mystical creatures, only rarely seen through the length of a connecting corridor. Other sightings were as small dots in the distance – girls having been dismissed ten minutes ahead of the boys at the end of the day to avoid any impropriety.

Mr Gover, an austere man, was the headmaster and the majority of teachers were émigrés from the Welsh Valleys. Discipline was strict and corporal punishment liberal for those who stepped out of line. The teachers were hard-working, though most of their energy and enthusiasm were targeted at the A-stream. If you were allocated to the lower streams, expectations were low and self-fulfilling. How many of these young minds will have failed to fully flower for want of a little individual support and encouragement? Fortunately, I made the top class and, without too much concern for my less favoured fellow travellers, began to thrive in the new environment.

A few months into the first term, chance and good fortune decided to take a further hand in an unexpected way. The journey to school entailed taking a bus to the centre of Romford and walking up through the market to Pettits Lane. The stalls were set up in the early morning on market days, and one in particular, selling second-hand books and manned by a plump chap with a cheery manner, caught my eye. I took to browsing the non-fiction titles for ten minutes or so as I passed by. As I perused the texts, I came to realise that here was a treasure trove of knowledge hitherto unimagined. For younger readers, it is probably difficult to envisage a world where the total sum of human knowledge is not accessible at the press of a computer key or touchscreen. Knowledge had to be actively sought through books and libraries, and finding a hidden source of cheap material on a market stall was exhilarating.

Like most boys of my age I had been given a chemistry set, and I think that the seeds of an interest in science were just beginning to germinate. On finding a number of advanced-level chemistry books, however, my thirst for knowledge exploded. My parents must have been perplexed as, during any spare moment, I sat with an open text of formulas and equations on my lap, consumed with interest and wonder. These days, as I struggle to remember my neighbour's name, it is difficult to recall the sponge-like qualities and innate curiosity of young minds. There was only one problem – although university texts, they were from the 1930s and, as I was later to find, lacking in new insights and advances. My parents, however, must have recognised that an important spark had been kindled because, on a very tight budget, they purchased a subscription for a fortnightly science magazine that accumulated to become an encyclopaedia.

As my range of interests evolved, the book titles became more diverse: *A Primer on Organic Chemistry*; *The Biochemical Basis of Metabolic Disease* (who would have thought that rare patients could excrete urine like maple syrup?!); *Science and Religion*. The age of the books could still cause problems, however. I found a book on bridge written by a notable expert, Eli Culbertson, in the 1930s. I became fascinated by the theory of the game and learnt his bidding conventions by heart. Little was I to know that this system had been

26

long superseded and, when I later came to play the game, I was surprised that my confident bidding was met with astonishment and disdain.

My favourite fictional book at the time was entitled *The Wolf Patrol*, and I returned to it frequently. It is a tribute to Baden-Powell's recently formed Scout movement by John Finnemore, and is a ripping yarn set around the turn of the twentieth century. I found it in a dusty bookcase at Nanny Alice's house rather than on the market stall. The two main characters are Chippy, a streetwise ragamuffin from the other side of the tracks, and Dick, a middle-class boy who befriends Chippy and attends a grammar school. Dick's uncle is persuaded to set up a Scout group and Chippy is invited to join. Today this act would be about embracing inclusivity, social awareness and acceptance of diversity. In the book, I think it is because Dick is a good egg. A strong bond evolves during a series of schoolboy adventures as the social barriers between them gradually dissolve. Chippy teaches Dick how to bake a 'toothsome' hedgehog in a ball of clay to remove the prickles, masterminds the defeat of a rival Scout group in a 'war game' by a mixture of street cunning and devious rule-breaking, and shows valour in saving a young child almost lost in a swirling millpond. The resonance is obvious, and no subtle explanations were needed to account for my love of this book.

The intake of Pettits Lane School was very much white working class, and I have very few recollections of any other ethnic groups being represented in the school. Perhaps this is why I don't remember witnessing any episodes of racism in my childhood. That is certainly not to say that the seeds of the subliminal and institutional racism of later years were not fermenting below the surface, or that the casual racism of the more dubious television sitcoms of the 1970s did not reflect attitudes in some quarters. An Indian family did move close by in Jutsums Lane, but they seemed to become well integrated into the local community. One son, who we called Danny, was accepted into our little gang of friends at primary school without question and we made every effort to help him with his faltering English. The openness and innocence of children remind us that no one is born with an innate suspicion of 'the other'. I met Danny many years later at a bus stop when visiting my mother, and he was wearing a pinstripe suit. He told me that he had a successful career as an accountant and I felt a kinship. We would both prove that it was possible to break through the social barriers of the time, but even two swallows do not make a summer.

Alan was a quietly spoken and gentle boy whom I had grown to like in my first few weeks at Pettits Lane School. Sandy-haired and slight in build, he tended to sit with the less exuberant and extrovert lads towards the front of the class so that his short-sightedness did not impair his ability to see the blackboard. I moved to the left and then the right before hitting him full in the face, and followed with another blow to his left temple. He stumbled slightly, took a deep breath and stood his ground.

Boxing was mandatory in PE lessons at the school, and there was no hiding place for the faint- or weak-hearted. It could easily have been me on the receiving end as there were two brothers in our year who boxed at the National Schools Championships. Perhaps my southpaw stance gave me some advantage since there was little attempt to match physique or expertise, and generally I felt that I gave as good as I got, providing I avoided the pugilist siblings!

With the foolhardy but ultimately courageous example of my father in the South China Sea, I had decided on a policy of putting my hand up to volunteer for any opportunity on offer at the new school – sporting or otherwise. And so it came to be that I was listed for the first bout (very lightweight!) at the school boxing tournament. My father dutifully attended.

Keith, my opponent, was sharp, streetwise and had done a bit of boxing before. I thought I did OK, but I was not in his class and the judgement went against me. Still, as my father put a consoling hand on my shoulder, I sensed a trace of pride. My disappointment in defeat was tempered by the thought that I may have just gone up a small notch or two in his estimation.

My boxing career was short-lived, but the annual school tournament somehow survived despite my absence. Held in November, it remained a sporting highlight and drew in a good audience of parents and town folk. Later, as a prefect in the fourth year, a number of us were requested to police the school to ensure that visitors did not stray or cause mischief. We took this very seriously as we performed our security sweeps in the dark and silent building. At the end of the evening, we returned to the hall and were unexpectedly met by a subdued audience and an atmosphere of tension laced with a hint of threat. At the height of the Cold War, news had just filtered through that President Kennedy had been assassinated. In later years I would have an excuse to give an exaggerated description of my boxing career whenever I was interrogated at dinner parties about where I was when Kennedy was shot.

"Down!" shouted my Uncle Joe as he lifted the twelve-bore shotgun to his shoulder and let off both barrels. The deafening boom left me with ringing ears for a moment or two, but the duck had escaped and Tessa, his Labrador gun dog, looked disappointed.

My Aunt Dorothy had met and married Joe in the mid 1950s when my mother was in Black Notley Sanatorium. This was not well received by my mother, who felt a modicum of betrayal after caring for her younger sister as she grew up. Indeed, it would contribute to their virtual estrangement in later years.

Joe was from a poor farmworker family in South Essex and his country accent, social awkwardness and limited schooling successfully hid his innate intelligence. He worked as a builder and was 'a bit of a tearaway' as a youngster but, in later years, his generosity, kindness and warmth shone through. Always something of a joker, family anecdotes were never complete without descriptions of the time a stray spark entered his inadvisable pocket of fireworks on Guy Fawkes Night. He tore off his jacket with some speed as the pyrrhic spectacle unfolded. Or the time we set off in his Morris Ten to go to a family gathering. We had travelled a short distance when Joe disappeared from the driver's seat – only one hand on the wheel and a foot on the accelerator remaining. I heard the muffled cry of "Bloody hell" from the absent driver. His door had not been secured and Joe was more out than in as he struggled to maintain control of the swerving car. Of course, each of these events could have ended in injury or worse, but somehow he always survived, surfacing with a broad grin on his weathered face as another anecdote was added to the family archive.

He was devoted to my Aunt Dorothy and eventually they set up home in a caravan on the edge of a moat, and in the grounds of a former rectory-cum-country-club. The caravan was surrounded by fields and apple orchards, and although this unconventional arrangement was frowned on by my mother, I was allowed to stay with them for short periods in my teenage years. They were never to have children, but Joe had a natural warmth with youngsters and I was treated like a surrogate son. To a young 'townie', this was heaven, particularly since we could afford few holidays at the time.

For Joe, guns were part of his country heritage and he owned a number apart from the twelve-bore, including a 410 poacher's gun and a high-powered air rifle. He taught me to handle them safely and I didn't have a moment's self-doubt when my aunt agreed to my requests to take one or other on sorties round the orchard. I mainly targeted inanimate objects, but on one occasion, and more by luck than skill, I killed a blue tit. The remorse was so overpowering that I think the Essex birdlife was safe from my attention for evermore. In later life, it would seem remarkable – and a little disconcerting – that I had had the freedom to access guns at such a young age. Certainly, I would be horrified if my children or grandsons made similar requests in these safety-conscious times. On the other hand, the experience gave me a sense of responsibility and self-reliance: character-building, providing one survived.

The Swinging Sixties were a background hum during my years at Pettits Lane School. Although we were only a dozen miles from Carnaby Street and the Abbey Road Studios, this had little practical impact on the parochial pattern of my teenage life in the suburbs. To grow up in the '60s, however, was to be surrounded by an ambience of optimism and hopefulness which can be barely recognised in the cold, cynical, high-tech world of today. Post-war, there was a new social order and the baby boomer generation was coming! Anything could be achieved and there really was a sense that the country could move to a better place. Colours were brighter, youth was making its mark on the world and there was music the like of which had never been heard before. Of course, we were too young, innocent and afraid of consequences (before the contraceptive pill) for the sex, and too poor, naive and nervous of authority figures (including our parents) for the drugs. The music, however, provided a constant soundtrack to the times – and we were so spoilt for choice. The Liverpool Sound, led by the Beatles, of course; British blues bands; new-wave heavy rock; electric folk; Motown; the richly orchestrated pop of the Moody Blues and odd idiosyncratic artists like Jethro Tull and Captain Beefheart. And this list only scratched the surface as we became submerged in a sea of mesmerising sounds.

It was always necessary to listen to a new Beatles song three times. The first to dispel the horror: "That's it – they have really lost it this time, complete rubbish!"

On the second spin, however, a melodic apparition would appear through the musical mist: "Hang on, there is something going on here…"

And by the third: "Wow! That is amazing! I have never heard anything like it – you've gotta listen to this!"

There was just the odd exception to this sequence. *Tomorrow Never Knows* hit me in the midriff and made my head spin on first hearing with a sense that music would never be the same again.

On the other hand, having access to music was another

matter. I certainly did not have the money to purchase records. In the early '60s, we relied on Radio Luxembourg, which was weakly transmitted from the Continent and drifted in and out of reception. We listened on tinny transistor radios beneath the bedsheets so that the latest hits could be discussed over the lunch table the following day. The pirate radio station Radio Caroline was moored in the Channel and began broadcasting in 1964, but they were initially short of funds and records. I remember my early excitement was rapidly tempered by having to endure *Anyone Who Had a Heart* by Cilla Black every half-dozen plays. Later, I would be able to go to occasional live gigs and, though not recognising the iconic moment at the time, watched the Rolling Stones perform in Hyde Park. For an annual school dance, we booked a little-known group called the Foundations, a British soul band. In the time between booking and the dance, they released *Baby, Now That I've Found You*, which rapidly reached number one in the hit parade. Whether due to goodwill or contractual obligations, they turned up and gave us all a night to remember. Over the next couple of years, I was able to listen, transfixed, to the vocals of Joe Cocker and Sandy Denny and the soaring guitar of Paul Kossoff – each leaving an indelible mark on my memory. There can be little left to say about the cultural impact of '60s music, but without doubt it had a major influence on our young lives.

We were innocents abroad as teenagers in the '60s compared to those growing up in recent times. Before the summer holidays, we would plot out a detailed timetable of football in the park, tennis at local courts, or free time to hunt for newts in a farmland pond or grass snakes on rough ground by factory depots. For a treat at weekends, a small group of friends and I would purchase Red Rover tickets which allowed unlimited travel to all parts of London on the bus. On a whim, we would choose to travel to exotic-sounding destinations at the ends of routes on the periphery of the city. Invariably, this would result in disappointment. On one occasion, we headed towards Ongar which, in our naive young minds, was deep in beautiful Essex countryside. Perhaps it was, but we would never find out since the bus terminated some way off at a dingy dirty cafe with a dubious, dank-haired owner. Eyed with suspicion by a sinister group of bikers, we returned rapidly to the waiting bus that had just delivered us to the desolate spot. At other times we would visit London Zoo, the Monument on the Thames Embankment or museums in South Kensington. Walking to the Science and Victoria & Albert Museums, we would stop to stare at the fine Georgian houses and grand Victorian hospitals decorating Fulham Road. One of these, the Royal Marsden Hospital, would have more than a passing significance in my later life.

As we turned fifteen we were allowed to have a can of beer when we met at each other's houses on a Friday night. Before video recorders or Sky boxes I would pre-tape the soundtrack of Peter Cook and Dudley Moore in episodes of *Not Only... But Also*, and we would replay them, collapse laughing together and learn some of the dialogue for repeating surreptitiously in class at a later date. Some of these episodes would be wiped by the BBC in the future, and it is a great regret that we didn't keep them.

Many would feel that cycling on modern city roads is too dangerous to contemplate and I would not argue with this view. For cyclists, there is little point in having the moral high ground if you are viewing it from six feet underground. Yet on the quieter roads of my youth we cycled everywhere locally. One week in the summer, my father decided to paint the outside woodwork of my nan's house in Elm Park, which was about three miles away. We cycled over each day and there was the unfamiliar opportunity to do 'man's work' together. At the bottom of the garden by the old Anderson shelter and close to the District Line embankment stood a pear tree. It had a solitary fruit hanging from a branch, just reachable, and it was a source of torment throughout the week. Finally, I had to succumb. Fortunately, on the last day, my mother brought my younger brother to meet us, which gave me the perfect scapegoat when my nan spotted the missing fruit. Well, I never claimed to be George Washington!

In our family the idea of breaking sweat in a spare bedroom on an amputated and forlornly static exercise bike would have raised eyebrows. My father did not have a car and cycles were essential transport for work and play. The mindless drudgery of artificial fitness programmes was something for the future and we all led active lives. Undernourishment may have been a problem for some in the post-war period, but the malnourishment of overeating and obesity was a rarity in our childhood. Dad taught us all to swim at Mawney Road Baths, and I remember watching him play football for the Post Office team at the local recreation ground well into his thirties. The union played an active role in the members' social lives; organising children's parties at Christmas and sports days at the newly opened Hornchurch Athletics Stadium. Dad was close to forty years of age when I watched him compete in a 440-yards race and give his all. Part sprint and part endurance, this is one of the most gruelling distances for an occasional runner.

The essence of life in a secondary modern school in the '60s is perhaps best captured by the contributions to our school magazine. Fortunately, I retained my copies of the biannual issues between winter 1960 and summer 1965, and they shine a nostalgic light on the interests, perspectives and concerns of our youth. Actually, the existence of a well-presented and professional-looking magazine in itself gives some insight into the philosophy of the school. In the absence of desktop publishing, this must have been no easy task for our English teacher, Mr Price. Whatever the challenges, the teaching staff were genuinely determined to make the best of their flock, an ethic which was unlikely to be driven by thoughts of merit points or career advancement.

These small fragments of social history, their pages now yellowed with age, contain the usual descriptions of school achievements by the head boy and house captains, and there are short vignettes describing individual successes within classes. Buried amongst the jokes, quizzes and catalogues of examination and school sports day results, however, are small pearls of wisdom reflecting the children's world view. Taking the summer 1965 issue as an example, a pupil in Class 3A wrote a thoughtful article on Early Bird, the first commercial communications satellite to provide direct contact for television and telephone communication between North America and Europe. A short piece entitled *What the Critics Say* gave opinions from pupils on their interpretation of *Lord of the Flies, On the Beach, Allan Quatermain* and *Word to Caesar*. There are descriptions of school visits including *A Tour of the Houses of Parliament, St Paul's and the Stock Exchange*. Many are quite detailed and well written; others more succinct and to the point. Here is M.D.G.'s contribution, *3B's Visit to the National Gallery*. I document it in its entirety:

> *The visit was on the whole, enjoyed by everyone concerned in spite of initial difficulties with a revolving door. Though certain deprecating remarks were passed about the newly acquired and very expensive Cezanne, the rotundity of Rubens' work proved a major attraction, as did "The Martyrdom of St. Sebastian". It is hoped that similar visits to other galleries will take place and that a greater understanding of Art shall result.*

I have little doubt that, given more space, the writer would have had much more to tell us about the theatre of the absurd, the cultural and fiscal values of the art market, sexual awakening and the sublime nature of divine faith.

Other more considered pieces were in the form of 'for' and 'against', with topics covering the perils of smoking, comprehensive education, the common market and nuclear disarmament, reflecting the concerns of the day. How times have changed! There was also room for niche interests like spear fishing, cacti and keeping budgerigars. My own contributions seem to be confined to pseudo-romantic poems, commonly ending with variations on a distant owl hooting in the night. I did, however, write a rather good description of my judo club, though my excessive enthusiasm may have provoked rather too much detail for the average reader.

The most telling section, however, is entitled Old Boys' Corner, listing the direction of life's travel for past pupils. Here is a small selection from the 1965 issue:

G.B. (1961). Works for Roneo Ltd and is now completing the final year of his drawing-office apprenticeship.

M.R. (1960). Now at Mawney Road Swimming Baths as an attendant. Recently gained the Bronze Medallion of the R.L.S.S.

P.D. (1962). Works as a capstan lathe operator. Thinking of emigrating.

J.R. (1964). Works in a greengrocer's in the Market Place. Likes his job and is doing well.

D.S. (1963). Shipping clerk in the City dealing with all items of export trade to all parts of the world. Delighted with his prospects.

R.B. (1963). In the Stock Exchange where he organises delivery of shares to brokers. Has his own office and telephone.

P.S. (1963). Late of Covent Garden, now of Spitalfields. Works as a cashier for a firm of growers. Starts at 4:30 a.m. and finishes at mid-day.

G.M. (1964). Apprentice toolmaker. Attends evening classes at the Hornchurch College of Further Education.

Craft, electrical and engineering apprenticeships were popular, and others became clerks in the City, draughtsmen, chefs or carpenters, or chose to join the services, predominantly the navy. There was also the occasional laboratory technician; a description which may have inflated the responsibilities of the job but was certainly in the frame as my career choice at the time.

Or I might have become a policeman. My parents bought a new

wireless and, exploring the outer reaches of the short wavelengths one day, I came upon communications from the Essex Police control room. The responses were encrypted and replaced by pips, but we listened for hours to the messages directing the officers to incidents around the county. Bolting horses in Braintree, a domestic in Dagenham, a burglary in Billericay. I learnt the codes for different sectors (R-for-Romeo for the Romford cars) and came to recognise the identity of the D-for-Delta vans carrying police dogs and the unmarked Q cars. On one occasion, there was a disturbance at the end of Jutsums Lane and we ran with excitement to the front bedroom to watch the police cars flash by. This illicit timewasting must have been illegal, and I hope there will be no repercussions from my admission of guilt for a crime fifty years ago.

Whatever my chosen career, it was quite clear that I would not become a joiner or carpenter. Woodwork was not a practical skill I had a natural gift for. Best described as a botcher, I lacked the patience or dexterity to saw along a straight line or produce a tight-fitting dovetail joint. The Huguenot branch of my mother's ancestors were craftsmen who turned wood, made furniture and fashioned the bone frames of fans. Her brothers in the East End inherited this affinity with wood, and so did my brother, who has built sailing boats and canoes. Like my father's genes for good looks, however, this inherited trait and Darwinian advantage passed me by. On one occasion I decided to create a tea tray. As I repeatedly attempted to cut the edges square, it gradually diminished in size until I decided that carrying a single cup and saucer on a tray was not worthwhile. With great effort I did manage to construct a crude rectangular box with a handle, which I presented to my father as a container for his shoe-cleaning kit. To his credit he received it with enthusiasm and gratitude. However, it was not an object that would have found pride of place on display at the parents' open evening, and I suspect that my father would not have been too keen on seeing it there either.

When it came to discipline, the teachers could in general be described as hard but fair. They were, after all, dealing with some pretty tough cookies. The threat of the cane undoubtedly kept more difficult cases in check, although of course this approach would be frowned on in the present day. Some teachers would have a number of 'persuaders' at their disposal which could offer different textures of pain; the thin, whippy swish for the hand or the thicker bamboo for the backside. This is not from personal experience, you understand. I only received admonishment on two occasions in my school career, curiously, both from music teachers. In primary school I was put outside the door for repeatedly looking at my watch in choir practice, which I thought was a fair exchange; and at Pettits I received a gentle slipper for gossiping when I should have been playing the ghastly recorder.

I was happy at Pettits Lane School and began to develop a degree of self-confidence. In no small measure, this was due to my interest in science and the general recognition amongst classmates that I was an 'expert in the field'. Of course, this meant that I had to tiptoe a fine line and not be seen as either a teacher's favourite, or boastful and conceited. I was keen not to be bullied. This was sometimes problematic; if a difficult question stumped the class, the science teacher would turn to me and expect an answer. On the other hand, I was never top of the form and only gradually rose from an overall position of eighth to fourth in the class during the five years.

Perhaps participation in sport provided protection from bullying. Team sport in particular gave a defensive barrier of group bonding and friendship; acting as a shield to prevent the bully isolating their vulnerable victim. It was a tough school and others used humour, aggression and obsequiousness for defence. Yet some were unexpectedly immune – like the small, fey boy with an overprotective mother who was accepted by all and taken under the wing of the more belligerent class members.

On Wednesday afternoons, pupils in the fourth and fifth years were given the opportunity to attend 'clubs' where extra work could be done to satisfy particular interests. Metalwork, woodwork, history, art and technical drawing were popular, but of course I was thirsting to join the science club. Unfortunately, it did not get off to a good start. I read of a simple method for making the volatile anaesthetic chloroform from common household ingredients, and for some inexplicable reason, the teacher succumbed to my request to set up the experiment. Of course, the inevitable happened and the laboratory was rapidly evacuated – fortunately before somnolence enveloped the class.

The kindness and support of those Pettits teachers was unwavering. Mr Webster often gave up his lunch hour to give me extra tuition as the exams approached. On one occasion, after receiving a small microscope for Christmas, I found a supplier of biological teaching material and a small vial containing amoebae, a unicellular organism, duly arrived. We spent a happy hour looking for the elusive species, but I have never been entirely sure that the specks we identified were anything more than dust.

It was probably about this time that the earliest inchoate seeds of a desire to become a doctor lodged in my consciousness. It is often said that those who enter medicine have a childhood background of personal or parental illness and our family experiences may have stimulated a nascent altruism. The old science books from the market stall also included some medical and nursing texts, which fascinated me, and I remember persuading my mother to order several issues of the *British Medical Journal* from the local newsagent's. Most of the articles were, of course, incomprehensible, though I recall one on the 'fainting game' – a dangerous manoeuvre whereby a person hyperventilates and then expires hard against pressure, usually by putting a thumb in the mouth. This was described in the context of its use by servicemen to feign illness, but in more modern times it has been recognised by children as a 'legal high' and a number of deaths have been recorded.

The impracticality of any such medical ambitions was clearly recognised, however. I recall our form teacher in the third year asking us to give our career preference. Successive pupils gave their choices, which were, on the whole, plausible, until he reached Michael.

"I would like to be a doctor," he said quietly.

Michael was a junior member of the St John's Ambulance Brigade, which had clearly sparked his interest, and, for all I know, he may have achieved his ambition. On hearing his response at the time, however, I silently dismissed it with pragmatic disdain. There was no way a Pettits boy could become a doctor.

It was a fine spring morning as the nights were becoming shorter and the winter frosts fast departing. The day began prosaically enough with a double maths lesson and the booming voice of Mr Beynon. We had lived in fear of this large, intimidating man in our earlier years, with his military moustache, tobacco-coarsened bellow and lethal swishing cane. As our form teacher in the fifth year, however, we grew familiar with his idiosyncrasies and he could no longer hide his kinder side and deep commitment to the education of his charges. I grew to have great regard for him, and later visited him during his retirement. Midway through the morning, our headmaster, Mr Gover, unexpectedly entered the room and we were slow to rise to our feet. To say the least, this was an unusual event and we stood with an air of hushed expectancy.

"Now, can I ask you who wishes to move to a grammar school to study A Levels after you leave in the summer?" he enquired.

I really can't recall any thoughts at that moment – in retrospect, it seemed to have been an entirely involuntary and impulsive response to add my raised hand to those of four others. I had never consciously considered this option, and certainly it had never been discussed with my parents. This pivotal moment is best compared to when my wife said yes to my tentative marriage proposal and, in an instant, the world changed.

After some due deliberations on the financial consequences, and to their eternal credit, my mother and father would later agree to the plan. Viewed from a modern perspective, this would be no great deal, but to my working-class parents in the '60s it was very new territory.

Following a brief interview with the headmaster of the local technical high school, passing four O Levels (the entry requirement) suddenly became an imperative rather than an aspiration. Our teachers did their very best to furnish pupils with mathematics and English language, but anything on top was a bonus. I expected to pass the chemistry exam with a good grade and needed a further one or more successes in history, geography and technical drawing. When the results arrived and I had achieved my goal of four passes, I was strangely deflated. As I was joining a class where everyone else had seven or eight, five O Levels would have given me so much more confidence and credibility. But I was on my way.

Margaret Ayres with Betty in the Kent hop fields

Betty (sitting) at Black Notley tb sanatorium

George Standen

Betty Daltrey

Graham and Betty

George between Betty and Dorothy at Southend

David, John (Senior), Alice, Graham,
George and Dick Standen

Graham (left) with brother, Rod (sitting) and cousins at Grays

Dorothy and Joe wedding 1956

3

A New Beginning

I entered the sixth form of the high school in September 1965. There were two streams, one for science and one for arts. The first shock to overcome was the presence of girls. Admittedly, in my science class there were just two, but the effect was discombobulating for a lad who had rarely made human contact with such an alien species. My intention was to study physics, zoology and chemistry at A Level, but first I needed an O Level in the former. It was determined that I should have an intensive period of study and sit the exam in the November. I passed by the skin of my teeth and embarked on the three sciences, though the delayed start meant that I needed a third year to complete my A Level physics curriculum. I don't recall any major problems being accepted by the already well-integrated class of new colleagues. My turbulent early years were perhaps now paying dividends in terms of resilience and adaptability. In addition, securing places in the football first eleven and the tennis team catalysed close kinship in the heat of battle. New routines were established and I settled into a pattern of hard work and play for the time I was in the school.

The shock of hitting the ice-cold water of the lake took my breath as I jumped into the void and submerged beside the rowing boat. Trying to make sense of my surroundings in the soft green light filtering from the surface, I took a moment to orientate before setting off to swim beneath the hull. In retrospect, however, it would have been more advisable if I had jumped off the other side of the craft, as a firm breeze was drifting the boat in my direction of travel and I was making little headway. For a brief moment, I thought that this was not going to end well as I struggled for breath, but eventually I surfaced on the other side with a splutter. A forty-metre swim to shore, pulling a canoe, completed the swimming test.

We had travelled overnight from London to the Lake District and I had managed little, if any, sleep. The test in Lake Coniston was at 9am and it was certainly an effective wake-up call. As a group of sixth-form pupils on an outward-bound course, we camped in fairly primitive conditions on the side of the lake. Robert and I were late additions to the group; I think to make up the numbers. He was one of the quiet and thoughtful members of the class and, like me, not assimilated into the brash, confident and extrovert set that we had travelled with. We were both studying zoology in a group of five pupils who were avoiding the rigours of advanced-level maths. We had previously struck up a friendship, and gradually his hidden depths were teased out from behind the quiet persona. He was deeply interested in natural history and had a wall of aquaria containing exotic tropical fish in his bedroom. As the harlequin shards darted in and out of the weeds and rocks, we gossiped about school and talked of our hopes and dreams for the future. Robert also had a useful contact in the pathology department of a local hospital, and I still recall the formalin-preserved specimens we were shown after he arranged a visit. The intestine of a young girl containing a hairball, the blackened lungs of smokers containing tumours, and hearts distended in the end stage of failure.

We separated off from the main group one day and went searching for sundews in the sphagnum moss at the summit of the Old Man. On another, we hitched to a freshwater biology institute after Robert had arranged a visit. Even now, I'm surprised by our resourcefulness, and our biology teacher would have been proud. Despite our independent adventures, however, we were still able to take full part in the activity schedule of sailing, canoeing and hillwalking. On the penultimate day, bright and sunny, we set off as a group to traverse the lake in canoes. Inevitably, the weather did not hold and a squalling storm appeared in the distance before barrelling down the lake towards us. Waves broke over the open two-man canoes, and we began to take on water. For the second time in the week, a sense of unease descended, but we managed to reach the safety of the far shore with the loss of just one paddle. On our last day, we headed for Ambleside to meet the evening coach. Wandering the lakeside streets, we came across a television shop with a set silently projecting images in the window. It was the 30th July 1966, and we watched Geoff Hurst score the final goal in the World Cup final.

On the 4th January 1967, Sir Donald Campbell strapped himself into the jet-engined hydroplane *Bluebird K7*. He was attempting to break the world water-speed record over a five-mile course on Coniston Water. The *K7* flipped over and broke up at a speed in excess of three hundred miles per hour, killing Sir Donald instantly. On hearing the news, I mused again on the nature of existence and mortality, and recalled the soft green light filtering below the surface of Coniston Water as I struggled for breath.

Local historians tell us that a market has been present in Romford since 1247 and was a meeting place for sellers of livestock and grain in Essex and buyers from London. Although my memory only extends back to the early 1950s, I still recall pens containing sheep and cattle, and poultry being sold on this site. Livestock trading ended in 1958, but the market remained at the hub of the town. For a short time in the sixth form I worked on a stall selling general hardware and everything for the handyman. Philip, a classmate, arranged for me to work with him on the stall, which was rented by his father. It was another opportunity to experience a different work environment, but it was an early start and I soon found that the Saturday job sapped my energy and interfered with my schoolwork.

Phil had suffered poliomyelitis as a child and was left mildly disabled. In our childhood, closure of the paddling pool in the local park was a sign that a polio epidemic was imminent. Before a vaccine became available, this virus infected a significant proportion of the population. The disease was asymptomatic in the large majority, or caused flu-like symptoms from which the patient recovered fully. Such silent transmission meant that it could disseminate widely in the community. In one in two hundred cases, however, nerve paralysis of the legs and, less commonly, other parts of the body occurred, which could be permanent. At least one affected child could be found in most schools and the disease must have been yet another anxiety for parents at the time. Following the development of effective immunisation by Salk and Sabin in the mid 1950s the disease has largely passed into history in the West, although, unlike smallpox, has yet to be eliminated worldwide.

The tension was rising amongst the small crowd surrounding the brick-red, dusty clay court. It was five games all in the final set, and Barry, my tennis partner at the high school, was fighting to bring the rubber level. We had reached the semi-finals of the National Schools Tennis Championships at Wimbledon and were playing a pair from the public school, St Paul's. The format was a two-man team with two singles and a possible deciding doubles. I was a player of modest ability and, after the first round or two, would invariably lose my singles match. But our cause could generally be salvaged by Barry, who was Essex's reigning junior champion at the time. In the deciding doubles, I could use my one weapon – a ferocious, flat, left-handed serve – to good effect. The rest could then be left to my partner!

In fact, we lost the semi-final, but it had been a good week. We had caught a glimpse of Dan Maskell, a famous BBC tennis commentator of the time, and were given a tour of the Centre Court. Though silent and deserted, one could sense the history and, in our mind's eye, picture the scene of famous finals days of the past: Rod Laver v. Chuck McKinley and Angela Mortimer v. Christine Truman in 1961, and Roy Emerson v. Fred Stolle and Maria Bueno v. Margaret Smith in 1964 were fresh in our memory.

I had begun playing tennis at Pettits in the third year with three friends. Peter was another lad who had been afflicted by polio, and this slightly impaired his movement around the court. However, he was sharp at the net, a praying mantis waiting to strike mercilessly at any loose return. Rod, John and I were able players, but we lacked any coaching and it would be difficult to describe our unhoned skills as silky or cultured. Nevertheless, we would meet each Sunday morning, whatever the weather, and enjoy the fun, exercise and companionship.

At first sight, tennis, with its middle-class, elitist overtones, was a curious sport to be popular at a secondary modern school. It was driven by the personal enthusiasm and encouragement of a single master, Mr Clifford Thomas. Each year, he would enter Pettits into the Nestlé National Tennis Ladder Tournament. This took the form of a league table, but measured achievement by the number of games played rather than the standard or skill of the competitors. Its objectives were laudable: to promote the number of people taking part and encourage participants to play more games. In 1964, we were the top school in the country and were rewarded with a trip to London to meet some famous players including the Australians Bob Hewitt and Fred Stolle, and Diedre Catt, a successful UK women's champion of the time. We all received glossy tennis annuals, which the stars generously signed. The male pair won numerous Grand Slam doubles finals but, in the era of the great Roy Emerson, Fred Stolle was to become notable for losing six singles finals. There is a well-known photograph (amongst tennis history buffs!) of him striking a pose of absolute dejection on court, and I remember him saying to me with a quizzical smile, "Why am I always asked to sign this picture?"

I later joined a local tennis club, but was yet to feel fully comfortable crossing the social divide. The young members were friendly and welcoming, and I have to accept that any barriers were more likely to have originated in my head rather than theirs. At another local club I was employed during the summer to prepare the clay courts each afternoon ready for the arrival of members in the early evening. Like a shire horse pulling a plough, I dragged a mat across the courts to smooth the scuffs, swept the lines and regulated the sprinklers to dampen the clay. Mingling with the company directors, estate agents and accountants, my old clothes and covering of red dust and perspiration did nothing to enhance my social confidence.

I was also to follow in my father's footsteps, and began playing football regularly. You will not be surprised to know that, in addition to the dark good looks and battlefield heroics, he played centre forward for a top combined services team. He had trials with Portsmouth FC, who were in their pomp at that time, winning both First Division titles and FA Cup finals. The story goes that he was on the verge of signing, but the Royal Marines blocked his release. Of course, before the elimination of the £20-per-week maximum wage in 1961, a successful soccer career in the '40s would not have led to the riches of today.

I came to the attention of the football coach at the high school when, after being drafted into a house team as a makeweight, I acquitted myself well, marking a lad who played for the first eleven. For several years I played for the highly successful school first team and we rarely lost a match. Mind you, my modest contribution was likely assisted by the presence of a West Ham Colts centre forward, three county players and the future captain of the London University team. Our egos were deflated, however, when a game against a team of old boys was arranged to celebrate the opening of a new sports pavilion. Our opponents included a professional player from Romford FC, who were in the Southern League, a level below the old Fourth Division. He waltzed through our defence as though we were stationary cones on a training ground, and we learnt a valuable lesson. Unless you are Roger Federer or Lionel Messi, you will always encounter someone in life who is just a little bit better – but don't let it dampen your childhood hopes and aspirations. Follow your passion and don't live a life of quiet regret. And above all, don't be defeatist like my friend Simon, who was crestfallen on his eighteenth birthday when he came face-to-face with the harsh reality that he was never going to play for Spurs. When the Celestial Sports Master gives his final end-of-life report, he will say, *Does not let lack of skill, guile and subtlety dampen his enthusiasm. Tries hard and does his best with the limited tools available.*

There was one curious episode at the high school which was at once slightly comical and also a touch sinister. Those teaching the parallel sixth-form arts class had arranged a debate loosely based on political parties with a ballot at the conclusion. On hearing this, our chemistry teacher, who was well respected and had a dash of charisma, made a passing wry comment that he would vote for "Sir's Progressive Party" (or SPP). He probably didn't expect the consequences.

Like a wildfire travelling through a parched forest, and with our imagination captured, SPP stickers appeared on bags, chants were heard along corridors, posters adorned walls and informal committees were hurriedly formed in the common room. A general meeting was arranged which large numbers attended, and the SPP won by a landslide. If the party had developed any policies then I'm sure they would have been for the common good. But in retrospect, this rapid evolution of groupthink, begun by a charismatic 'leader' and with devotion to a cause, was a perfect example of how a movement with more malign intentions could take hold in society. I hope the arts teachers and pupils absorbed this take-home message from their hijacked political project.

Christmas was always a memorable time for our family. Dad was working double shifts until Christmas Eve, but Mum made it special, in part, I'm sure, as a reaction to her deprived childhood. For me, it is the mosaic of smells heralding the magic day that still persist. The aromatic fragrance of sap from the Christmas tree, the smell of mince pies that my mother only made at Yuletide, and it was not unknown for us to roast chestnuts on a rusty shovel on our open coal fire; a perilous activity that was significantly less romantic than the saccharine song lyric. On the last day of term, I had a ritual of taking the *TV Times Christmas Extra* into school to plan the family's viewing.

As the childhood wonder subsided in the late teenage years, a new tradition replaced the old – working at the Post Office. Three circuits a day, I cycled round unfamiliar streets in all weathers to collect letters and cards from boxes. My father was working nights and so I didn't see him, but there were no surprises in the warm responses I received from his colleagues when I told them I was George's son. I had a brief hint of how nepotism works in the City and the professions when my father managed to wangle me softer jobs in later years; accompanying drivers in vans and, on one occasion, simply ticking all my fellow temps in and out on the time sheet. It was nice to be in the warm, but the feather bed seemed strangely uncomfortable.

At the end of the two years, I was moderately successful in my chemistry and zoology A Levels; sufficient to apply for a place on all but the most competitive university courses if I worked hard on my physics in the third-year sixth. Normally, the high school had a good academic record – but not that year. The reason was obscure, but may have been related to the temptations of the sixth-year common room. In the absence of policing by teachers, classmates wasted time on smoking and playing cards and snooker, and they lacked the maturity and self-discipline to apply themselves to private study. More tempting to listen to a talented classmate bash out Beatles tunes on an old piano downstairs, which was fine for a social club but not good preparation for the new Cambridge Nuffield A Level syllabuses.

There were also many temptations outside of school in the late '60s and, of course, hormones were kicking in and girl- and boyfriends were a distraction. I don't want to suggest that I felt any schadenfreude – I didn't. I had made many good friends amongst my classmates. However, the confident set who borrowed their mothers' Cortinas and feigned sophistication had received a sharp reminder from the real world. Success had to be worked for. The end result was that, in a diminished field, I was chosen to be deputy head boy. This suited me fine – all the status of a white badge, but managing to avoid the work of the head boy at school functions and Speech Day. A further consequence was that many of the class would need to continue in the sixth form to retake their A Levels and I would be accompanied in my studies by unexpected fellow travellers.

I don't remember the precise moment I decided to apply to study pharmacy at university, or whether others influenced my choice. Nevertheless, it was a logical conclusion, combining as it did my interests in chemistry and medical science. It was also versatile, with a number of alternative career options available in the future. These included retail and hospital pharmacy, and more specialised scientific work in the laboratories of pharmaceutical companies. With a good degree, it might even be possible to study for a higher qualification. Any thought that I might study medicine was again rapidly dismissed. I was never going to achieve the high grades at A Level required, and in many cases a modern language at O Level was also needed. Indeed, it was only a few years before that Latin O Level had been mandatory. My extracurricular activities were also very limited. To this day, applicants to medical courses will almost inevitably have Grade 8 in two instruments, play in a youth orchestra, and fence or play rugby or netball for England. In between, they will have found time to visit the Third World and dig wells or build schools. I could offer none of these things. I also lacked the most powerful driver for admission at that time: a family member in the profession.

Then, as now, prospectuses from different institutions were requested. Nottingham seemed to offer a good course and, to be honest, the city was just the right distance from Romford. In those days of maintenance grants for living expenses and no course fees, this was a common criterion for making the university choice and certainly few sixth-formers wished to continue living at home. Now, the high cost of study excludes many from being able to flee the nest and it would be difficult to argue that this has had a beneficial effect on our youngsters' personal development.

With the application form duly completed and Nottingham at the top of the preference list, the day of the interview arrived. Alighting at the city's railway station and travelling by taxi to the campus, I entered through the north gate – and that was it, really. It was love at first sight. I was smitten by the rolling green fields of the parkland site with modern halls of residences dotted round the periphery, the more austere facades of the older Portland and Trent Buildings presiding over a picturesque lake, and the metropolis of 'Science City' at the bottom of the hill. There were pavilions, a lido, a health centre, sports facilities and libraries. In later years, some of my contemporaries would find the environment claustrophobic. There was also an argument that the self-contained 'shining city on the hill' was isolated from the surrounding population rather than part of the community. It was, after all, just a few miles from St Ann's, which at that time contained some of the worst slum housing in the country. To a young man who had a very limited view of the world outside of Romford, however, the impact was intoxicating. In a vague sense, I also had a strange feeling that I had come to a place that felt like my real home. This text is not about to descend into magic realism, but perhaps I had a premonition that Nottingham would be 'my' city, on and off, for the next fourteen years, and that these would be some of the happiest times of my life.

4

Pills, Potions and Ointments

To cut a long story short, a C grade in physics would secure a place on the pharmacy course at Nottingham, and a C grade was duly achieved. At the beginning of October 1968, my classmate Malcolm and I set off up the M1 in his orange-and-white hand-painted Morris Minor. He dropped me off in Nottingham before continuing on to Lancaster University to begin a degree in chemistry. We were, of course, determined to look the part. Not wanting to look out of place so soon after the Summer of Love, I had acquired a maroon velvet corduroy shirt discarded from the geriatric ward stock cupboard, ice-blue flares bought by my mother from Littlewoods, and a paisley-patterned neckerchief fashioned from old curtain material. The jeans were embarrassingly new, but there would have been hell to pay if I had blotched them with bleach or wantonly taken scissors to the knees to fully comply with the uniform. I had a place in Cripps Hall of Residence on the university campus, which provided a protective arm around the shoulder for an innocent away from home.

It could be argued that the first few weeks of university life hardly promoted a healthy attitude towards the discipline of study. There were no lectures for the first week as the students were allowed to find their feet, become familiar with their surroundings and settle into their accommodation. Various social events and gigs were put on in the Students' Union; clubs, societies and sports teams advertised for members; and many revelled in their new-found freedom away from home. For some, the fun-palace lifestyle proved an irresistible siren call for the remainder of their university careers – which were usually short! So-called Freshers' Week was soon followed by the Goose Fair in October. Dating from the thirteenth century, and still one of the largest fairs in the country, its name originally derived from the large number of geese which were driven from the flatlands of Lincolnshire to the Nottingham markets. After a short interlude, everyone was ready to embrace Rag Week with similar distractions from the main task. Eventually, however, the reality of academic work could no longer be resisted.

The pharmacy course was composed of four main subjects. Firstly, medicinal chemistry, which is concerned with the design and chemical synthesis of drugs in the laboratory. With my long-held interest in chemistry, I was delighted to explore this topic in greater detail. Secondly, pharmacology, which examines how drugs exert their therapeutic effects by interacting with biochemical processes in the cells of the body and through receptors and signalling pathways, and also how the chemical structure of the drug influences the duration of onset, therapeutic action and elimination of the agent. Thirdly, pharmacognosy, which specifically involves the study of drugs from plants – for example, digoxin derived from the foxglove and used in heart failure, and the *Vinca* alkaloids used in leukaemia treatment, which are extracted from the periwinkle. Overlapping medical therapeutics, these areas would have obvious appeal. I avidly absorbed the lecture material and bought additional textbooks to enhance my knowledge.

The fourth subject was pharmaceutics, which covered the application of physical chemistry to methods of drug delivery. For example, how various components of tablets, in addition to the active ingredient, influenced their stability, rate of dissolution in the stomach etc.; or how the physico-chemical properties of emulsions and creams enabled them to release drugs into the skin. In other words, the subject was more to do with the properties of the delivery system rather than the drug itself. One party piece by the lecturer involved demonstrating the difference between rheopectic and thixotropic liquids (stay with me here!). A rheopectic product has a thin consistency at rest, but under the stress of stirring or rapid movement, develops the increased viscosity of, say, thick hair gel. In a rare example of humour juxtaposing non-Newtonian fluid mechanics, the teacher would gently stir the liquid in a beaker in front of the class before suddenly flinging it towards the room in the manner of a clown with a bucket of confetti. The liquid remained in the pot, but this would have a sobering effect on the students slumbering in the 9am lecture, who exhibited the 'startle reflex' in unison! Of course, it was important that the lecturer did not confuse the beakers and perform the trick with the thixotropic solution – which had exactly the opposite properties. Remember this anecdote next time you squeeze toothpaste from a tube or apply ketchup to your meal; both are examples of thixotropic materials.

In general, this subject failed to ignite my enthusiasm and I approached the first lectures with resignation. However, my apathy proved no match for the force of nature that was a certain Dr Jones. Young and dynamic, he was, by a long way, the most inspirational teacher I had encountered and discharged purpose, energy and infectious enthusiasm like a nuclear reactor emits radiation. The pharmaceutics course required the submission of regular long essays on particular topics, and under his guidance I was inspired to visit the science library in the evening to explore the subject in greater depth and detail. On one occasion, I remember becoming totally engrossed by the factors influencing drug release from suppositories! On a more serious note, this was my first foray into the pleasure and satisfaction of research, albeit at the simplest level.

Now Professor Trevor Jones CBE, he would go on to have

a stellar career as director general of the Association of the British Pharmaceutical Industry, and serve on the boards of the Wellcome Trust as well as many major pharmaceutical companies, government agencies and the World Health Organization. I would like to think that he would be pleased and honoured to receive my lifetime award for most inspiring teacher along with his many other prizes and accolades. And I was very pleased to receive a £10 book token as the pharmaceutics prize at the end of my second year.

On the subject of suppositories, we were expected in those days to be able to formulate various pharmaceutical preparations in the laboratory – pills, potions and ointments – just in case we should ever secure a post at a branch of Ye Olde Apothecary Shop. Unfortunately, this was not my forte. My suppositories failed to set in the mould, my pastilles were hard and inedible, and my emulsions cracked. My wife maintains that I have used this as a long-standing excuse to avoid helping her with the cooking.

The social spectrum at Nottingham was wide; those from major public schools who failed to get into Oxbridge mingling with the unfamiliar lower strata, who were sometimes treated as an interesting species worthy of study. An exception was a young man a few doors up from me in hall who was born into a very well-known family of confectioners. He was tall, and even at a young age had the studied air of a patrician; his Marlborough vowels contrasting with my Estuary twang. However, he was a genuinely nice chap and we got on well. On one occasion, he was recounting a story about a conversation he had had with one of his neighbours about this or that.

"Who was the neighbour?" I enquired innocently.

"Oh, the Bishop of York," came the nonchalant reply, as though it was the most normal thing in the world. "He has an estate close to ours."

I was not sure that he was using the term 'estate' in quite the way I was familiar with.

63

Whether my new colleague completed his degree at Nottingham or whether the demands of the family company intervened, I cannot recall. I do remember, however, that I valued his friendship and also the occasional Chocolate Orange that came my way.

Early in my first term at Nottingham I met Dave at a football trial. We bonded in the shared commiseration of our failure to be shortlisted for the university seconds football team. I recognised a familiar accent and we agreed that we must have played football against each other at high school. For teenagers, this was ample reason to strike up a rapport. Fair-haired, slim and with boyish good looks, Dave had a more relaxed attitude to life than me, but seemed to genially accept my earnest streak as a minor character flaw. With his calm demeanour and gentle sense of humour, I decided early on that he was my alter ego who had an outlook to be envied. There may have been strong opinions and uncompromising attitudes below the surface, but they rarely disturbed his placid nature and, despite our contrasting personalities, our friendship has been enduring.

Come the vacation, it became clear where Dave's quiet charm and popularity were derived from. I drove over to meet his family and entered a house aglow with warmth and laughter. The central character was his mother, Babs, who radiated joyous good humour as she fussed over her brood. In addition to Dave, there were two attractive sisters who shared the perky exuberance of their mother. Meanwhile, his father, Jack, sat quietly in the corner with a benign smile, surveying the noisy chatter surrounding him. As a deputy head of a primary school he must have been adept at filtering out the hubbub of lively young voices. Periodically, groups of the sisters' friends would appear and contribute to the chaotic mix before the house emptied for a brief respite of calm. It has to be said that, coming from a household where the atmosphere could be quite oppressive at times, this experience was something of a culture shock, but I was welcomed with such warmth that the visits soon became an anticipated treat.

In the second year, Dave, myself and another friend, Alan, shared a modern, three-bedroomed detached house to the north of the city in Arnold. Quite how Dave managed to secure such impressive accommodation for £8 per week I'm not sure. Now a suburb of the city, Arnold was mentioned as a settlement in the Domesday Book and was later a staging post on the Great North Road as it travelled through Sherwood Forest on its path from London to York. It was notable in our time for producing Home Ales, and while living there I was reacquainted with the wafting aroma of hops. One disadvantage of our otherwise excellent accommodation, however, was that the heating by night came from storage heaters which were barely effective and beyond our means. On a particularly cold winter's day, Dave decided that we should light a fire and Alan and I were dispatched to chop up wooden crates in the garden. We laboured for an hour, periodically taking in the piles of kindling. Returning after the last of the planks had been splintered, we were just in time to see the final embers fading in the grate! Our friendship was again tested when, on the last day of spring term and just before we travelled home, Dave was persuaded by a door-to-door seller that it would be superb value to purchase a hundredweight of potatoes.

At weekends, we cooked for ourselves, which was a journey of exploration in itself. We were assisted by a sweet, red-haired girl at the local Sainsbury's checkout who seemed to take us under her wing. Dave's culinary confidence commonly exceeded his practical skills in the kitchen, but generally his offerings were edible. Indeed, we were all grateful to his aunt who had furnished him with a copy of *The Economical Cook Book* at the beginning of the year. There was only one complete disaster – in retrospect, sausages might have been a safer option than calf's liver, which we all agreed had the astringent flavour of antiseptic mouthwash. And we were careful to avoid explaining to our neighbour why we needed to borrow his stepladder the day after Shrove Tuesday and an overenthusiastic pancake-tossing competition.

Following the summer examinations, it was traditional for us to go to Skegness to have a beer and some innocent fun on the beach. We slept in the cars at an adjacent nature reserve, which added to the adventure. On the first occasion, however, Dave in particular slept very poorly, disturbed by the cold and his contorted posture. Thinking that, as a trainee pharmacist, I might know something about medicines, he requested advice and, not unreasonably, I suggested an antihistamine. After all, these drugs have a mild sedative effect. Unfortunately, like Dave's culinary skills, my confidence exceeded my therapeutic knowledge and I provided him with promethazine; an agent with a delayed onset but prolonged duration of action. He tossed and turned all night as usual, but enjoyed a very sound sleep all the following day as the rest of us frolicked on the beach. Re-establishing my medical credentials after this debacle was a long process.

Alan had purchased a new record player at the beginning of the year and I bought a handful of long-player vinyl discs by artists I couldn't resist: Pentangle, Free, The Nice, and Neil Young's first album. I sold them all at the end of the year so that I could purchase Goodman & Gilman, a massive tome on clinical therapeutics, for £7. It became my bible and followed in the grand tradition of ancient chemistry books, the *Contract Bridge Red Book on Play* and *The Wolf Patrol* as go-to texts for balancing on my knees in idle moments. Though it did have the added advantage of giving my quadriceps a good isometric workout at the same time. On the other hand, it might have been more sensible to use the money from the sale of the records to replace my shoes, which were becoming decrepit.

If I think of the Arnold house now, it is a perpetual Saturday morning bathed in sunshine and laughter with the beautiful chords of *Alone Again Or* from the *Forever Changes* album by Love drifting from the windows. In our future lives, we would rarely have a greater sense of freedom or more carefree spirit. Walt Whitman's poem *Song of the Open Road* would never be more apt as he used an American highway stretching to the horizon as a metaphor for the promise and optimism of youth. In the afternoon we might go off and kick a ball on an empty pitch we found in Ravenshead, or drive to Newstead Abbey along the Nottingham Road. The ruins of Byron's retreat were a favourite haunt where we could wander round the lakes and explore the pools, waterfalls and gardens in the manicured grounds. For me, the abbey had an almost spiritual draw and I headed there for celebration in good times and used it as a sanctuary in darker moments. An enchanted retreat which, during visits in later years, would never fail to transport me back to my younger self.

Returning to the subject of worn shoes, the local authority grant was awarded on the basis of a sliding scale depending on parental income. For an average working-class salary, the grant paid was just sufficient to survive without indebtedness. In theory, parents were obliged to make up the difference to the full sum, a so-called parental contribution, but this was not always easy to find for the hard-pressed. In common with many students, I worked all through the summer vacations and also Christmas on the post, but kept Easter free to prepare for examinations. As we have seen, holiday jobs, which were freely available, provided an education for life, limited the financial demands on the family during vacations, gave some self-respect and provided for a few extras, particularly if you wished to run an old car.

I had just finished reading the novel *Nausea* by Jean-Paul Sartre and I was as wise about its contents at the end as I was at the beginning. This was not surprising as I had the scantiest knowledge of existentialism and, indeed, of philosophical ideas in general. Nevertheless, I was on a drive to improve my general education. The crusade was stimulated by awareness that my own field of vision was narrowly limited to the sciences. Also, in hall, I was surrounded by arts undergraduates studying English, sociology, and politics, who seemed so much cooler and worldlier – and more successful with girls! I took to visiting the university bookshop and chose paperbacks from the literature section essentially at random. In some cases this was successful and authors such as Aldous Huxley and George Orwell were accessible and entertaining. Others, like D. H. Lawrence, I could appreciate but I'm sure I would have missed the nuances recognised on a creative writing course. And in those like Sartre; well, better luck next time.

On the other hand, the main character in *Nausea* did teach me a new word: 'autodidact', which I had to look up in the dictionary. *A person who is self-taught and without the benefit of formal teaching including teachers or educational institutions.* Wikipedia gives a useful list of famous autodidacts which includes George Bernard Shaw, Ernest Hemingway and Sir Terry Pratchett. With pompous self-regard, I could see a hint of the description in my sorties to the second-hand bookstall in my teens. A true autodidact would appear closer to home a few years later, however, in the form of my future father-in-law. Fred had a moderately deprived childhood and left school at fourteen to work as a points boy on the trams in Bristol. Later, he would become a bus conductor and, in a common theme, his life would be interrupted by the war. All the time, however, he was an avid reader of books, with an emphasis on history, economics and politics. Eventually, he would gain a place at Ruskin College, an institution supported by the trade unions and committed to providing educational opportunities for those with few or no qualifications. The list of alumni is very impressive and, as expected, includes many well-known Labour politicians. Here Fred would revel in the enthusing atmosphere of academia. At the end of the two years he had the opportunity to transfer formally to an Oxford University course, but financial considerations prevented it – to his lifelong regret. However, he would eventually make his mark as a teacher in special needs education, and his long road to self-improvement could undoubtedly be judged a success. His mind would remain sharp into his eighties, when I remember him quizzing me with mounting excitement on the application of new DNA techniques for tracking ancient populations across continents.

D. H. Lawrence was one of the few exceptional alumni of Nottingham University until a brace of the rare birds arrived in 2003. I enjoyed the visual imagery and poetic lyricism of his books. Along with the works of Alan Sillitoe, places in the immediate vicinity were vividly described and the characters spoke in the familiar dialect that we heard every day in the city. Visiting the villages of the Nottinghamshire coalfields, it was easy to transport yourself back to the working-class life of earlier times described in the texts. Mind you, D. H. Lawrence did cause me some problems in Romford on one occasion. I had taken to reading his books at home one vacation and decided, with the thoughtlessness of youth, to give my parents a lecture on his literary merits and how well he captured the essence of Nottingham life of the period. Unfortunately, Christmas 1971 was poor timing as they were in the middle of a discussion on how they would cope with a sudden drop in income inflicted by a forthcoming postal workers' strike. They were dealing with a drama in their own lives and my comments were quite rightly met with an icy stare before they carried on with their conversation.

Actually, there was a more serious aspect to this vignette. There was just a hint, an unspoken suggestion, that my parents had begun to feel that I was drifting away from the background we shared. They were not familiar with the life I was leading at university and, as I stood on the threshold of adulthood, they may have felt uncomfortable with who I might become. This impression was reinforced many years later when my Aunt Else, an indomitable Danish lady with unremitting good sense, told me that she had taken my mother to task because she had voiced her concerns over welcoming some of my university friends to Romford. My mother thought that they would be far too grand to entertain in our working-class home. She was unaware that the young man who found friendship and common bonds in a bubblegum factory was not about to change his character.

At this point it would be worthwhile taking a short detour to describe my Aunt Else in more detail. She married my father's younger brother, Dave, in 1957 and now, aged ninety-four at the time of writing, her mind remains sharp as a Viking blade. She was born to a comfortable and well-connected family on their farm in a village to the north-west of Copenhagen. The farm had a stud of fine thoroughbreds and she remembers the brother of King Christian visiting to purchase a horse and staying for supper. Later she would train as a chiropodist and take up practice in Copenhagen.

Denmark was invaded by the Germans in April 1940 and, given its small size, the resistance was short-lived. However, with time an effective network of underground fighters developed, supported by the British Special Operations Executive.

"And what did you do in the war, Else?" we recently enquired.

"We killed Germans," she replied tersely in her still-guttural accent.

For the briefest of moments a steely glint of anger and defiance replaced the warm, smiley face. Under the guise of her professional role, she acted as a courier for weapons, explosives and intelligence between different cells of the resistance. Senior operatives of the underground stayed in her flat, and she described on one occasion a leader returning with a bloodstained shirt.

"A German?" she enquired.

"No, a quisling," he replied.

She described how resistance fighters caught by the Nazis were kept in the upper storeys of the Gestapo building in the centre of Copenhagen, and that many files on potential collaborators were stored in the rooms below. Under pressure from the Danish underground, the British eventually launched Operation Carthage, a low-level raid by Mosquito fighter-bombers which destroyed the building towards the end of the war. Unfortunately, civilian casualties were high and eighty-six children and twenty adults were killed in a nearby boarding school. Some of the prisoners escaped and Else shielded a number in her flat – many showing signs of horrific torture. These stories put tales of school life in the '60s in the shade.

Else first met my Uncle Dave in Genoa in 1956 after travelling with her family to meet her brother, who was on a stopover in the port while travelling on the MV *Meonia* from Malaysia where he worked on a Danish rubber plantation. Dave had also been in Malaysia as an engineer for Babcock & Wilcox and was a passenger on the same ship. The couple met in a bar one evening and there was clearly a spark because, on returning to England, Dave immediately set off by car to visit Else in Denmark.

As my aunt finished her story, she added one final twist.

"And I looked after Niels Bohr's feet!" she remarked casually.

The Danish physicist and Nobel Prize winner was a regular client before fleeing to Britain towards the end of the war. He became an important member of the Manhattan Project, which produced the first nuclear weapons. My aunt may have taken good care of his feet, but the British and Americans were determined to take good care of his mind. My wife and I always had a strong connection with Else; indeed, she would step in to look after our two-year-old when her sister was being born and I was working long hours. If anything, our bond would become closer in the future as events unfolded.

I counted the pile of £10 notes a second time and it still came to £160.

This can't be right, I thought. Mr Connell, the senior manager, had directed me to the pharmacy office and asked me to double-check the takings from the till before the cash was taken to the night safe. He distinctly told me that the sum was £150, and I couldn't quite make sense of it.

I returned the cash and relayed my finding. He said nothing.

I'm sure the streetwise youngsters of today wouldn't be taken in by this ruse to test my honesty! I was working for a month in the Romford branch of Boots Pharmacy to gain experience in the retail side of the profession. To be honest, although I wasn't sure which area I would enter, it was never going to be retail pharmacy. But my general rule, particularly when it came to holiday jobs, was that no new experience was ever wasted. And the funds would always be useful.

I served on the proprietary (non-prescription) medicines counter with a young woman, Carrie. She had straight black hair; a melting smile; saucer-wide, flirtatious eyes; and a keen sense of self-awareness as a temptress. I was tantalised with tales of her older boyfriend who worked at Ford, drove a new Anglia and took her to nightclubs. She was friendly, but the unspoken inference was that I was outside her league – and she was right!

I actually enjoyed my month exchanging chirpy cockney chatter with the customers and hearing about their minor maladies. In the future, I would have the responsibility of providing care for patients with much more serious ailments and it was never too early to develop the necessary interpersonal skills.

At other times, I worked for Macarthy's, a central pharmaceutical distributor, where I was asked to check the large shipments of different drugs sent from individual companies. Deliveries were sporadic, which gave me ample time to read the package inserts of each preparation; a great way to consolidate my knowledge about their medical indications, dosages and side effects. In the pharmacy department of a local hospital, I printed out labels for medicines and helped make large batches of lotions, creams and ointments.

It strikes me now that, virtually without exception, everybody I encountered in a variety of holiday jobs showed warmth and kindness. It would be good to know that human nature has not changed and that temporary workers and interns are treated with the same level of goodwill in today's less forgiving environment.

Later, I would visit the shining capitals of Big Pharma: citadels of steel, glass and wealth bringing to mind the industrial dreamscapes of a Ballard novel; sinister, secretive worlds behind double-locked gates. A near contemporary became vice president of a major pharmaceutical company: executive dining, business-class travel, share options and well-resourced research facilities with the best equipment available. Who in their right mind would seek a different path?

In the third year of the Nottingham pharmacy degree we were allowed to specialise, and I chose pharmacology and medicinal chemistry. Roger, a PhD student in the department, acted as a demonstrator and assisted in our laboratory work. We struck up a friendship and it was not long before I was invited to his flat for a meal and to meet his delightful young wife, who was a nurse. Roger was a sweet, generous man who was very tall and thin with long fingers and a slightly fluted voice. One day, we were wandering around the lake on the university campus in late-summer sunshine, discussing our career paths, and he outlined his plan to transfer to a medical course following the completion of his doctorate. I told him that I had also considered this option but was deterred by the expense, the length of the course and the thought of endless exams in the future. He gently provided solutions to each obstacle and, for the first time, becoming a doctor moved from a dream to a potential reality. To this day, I owe a debt of gratitude to Roger for his wise counsel, even though he is no longer with us. Despite his reassurances, however, I did not have the courage to apply to study medicine at this stage. A number of other pieces of the jigsaw would have to be put in place first. As it happens, one of these pieces would enter my life in a month or two, but until then, my plan of progressing to study for a PhD remained in place. I had managed to secure a postgraduate position at the Institute of Cancer Research in Sutton, Surrey, providing I achieved a good first degree.

At risk of sounding trite, I thought that I had begun to find a sense of direction and purpose during my three years in Nottingham. As finals approached, and back in Cripps Hall for the third year, a feeling of transition was in the air. When it came to exams I had an unsophisticated approach to preparing for them. Unlike arts subjects, where one had to actually think, reason, compare and contrast, look for subtlety and nuance, and carefully plan answers, I would simply apply strong-arm, or at least strong-wrist, tactics. Three weeks before, I would begin writing and rewriting my lecture notes until they were committed to memory. True, I had always kept good course notes and liberally sprinkled them with additional information from outside sources. For me, however, it was simply a means to an end and I was never under any illusion that the outcome reflected intelligence or high levels of erudition. As I left the examination hall for the last time after the fifth and final paper, I breathed a sigh of relief: no more exams – ever! Well, that would eventually come true but, as it turned out, nearer the age of forty rather than twenty!

I was sitting on my bed, decent but damp after a shower, when Claire and Eileen appeared at the door a week or two later.

"Graham, we have been up to Trent Building – you have got a first!"

I broke all the rules of etiquette concerning girls on your course and gave them a hug. My immediate response, I think, was a sense of relief. It would be wrong to say that I didn't have a moment of elation and a more studied sense of achievement later, but it was in my nature to focus on looking forward rather than back. I was very soon thinking about the next stage and the notion that my plan to move to London could be finally put in place.

The sense of transition heightened, and we began clearing our rooms for the last time. We would stay in touch with some close friends, while others would become memories fading with time. We had taken all that Nottingham had to offer and we were ready to move on. With a week to go before the end of the summer term, we were preparing to say our last goodbyes.

And then I met my future wife! My roommate and his girlfriend planned a celebratory meal and asked a friend along. A makeweight was needed to make up a four, and preferably one with a car. And so I first met Lin, the proud new owner of a 2:1 degree in history. Navy hot-pants suit, long blonde hair, grey-green eyes; like the girl on the Boots counter, she might be out of my league. At the end of the evening, as I dropped her home, she slipped a pound note in my shirt pocket to cover her share of the cost. That was it – I definitely had to see this girl again! Love at first sight? At the risk of sounding ungallant, I don't think either of us would admit to that. Our minds were too scrambled by finals and we were far too sensible. However, we probably both felt that something serious was going on and that here was a potential keeper.

We spent the entire week together in a whirlwind romance. On the way to an evening walk at Newstead Abbey, I stopped the car to rescue a hedgehog running haphazardly across a roundabout. I'm almost 100% sure that this was done in the best interests of the hedgehog rather than as a devious attempt to impress my new girlfriend with my sensitivity. We had a sophisticated meal at a Berni Inn and walked hand in hand around the university lake before the week culminated in Dave's twenty-first birthday party in the Lakeside Pavilion. At the end of the seven days, though, as we edged towards returning home to Romford and Bristol, an important decision had to be made.

5

Teenage Preoccupations

Neurobiologists and developmental psychologists tell us that adolescence is a time of rapid change and adaptation in the human brain. In teenagers, these alterations can lead to a range of abnormal feelings, emotions and behaviour. Learned articles argue that this accounts for their sensation-seeking, egocentricity, risk-taking and impulsiveness. It is also a time when adolescents often become preoccupied with the great questions and mysteries of life, like politics, religion – and how to impress members of the opposite sex! As a child of the '60s, I didn't seem markedly out of step with my peers, but we must have been puzzling to our parents at times.

There were no surprises for me on the political front, with my parents and background strong determinants of my direction of travel. Having said that, neither of my parents were ragingly political or left wing, although they could never bring themselves to vote Tory. My father was a strong union man, but odd comments showed that he had a clear eye when it came to their excesses. He knew the world was a complicated place and there were always several ways of looking at things. I had the certainty of youth. To me it was self-evident: industrial decline in the '60s could be traced back to the decay of Macmillan's government, and Labour, led by Harold Wilson, was thwarted by the Establishment and poor managers who spent their time on long liquid lunches and afternoons at the golf club. Meanwhile, the Oxbridge set pulling all the levers met at Ascot and Henley to quietly plan their next assault on the working class. With youthful brio, I announced to the family in my late teens that quite clearly there should only be a threefold difference in levels of income in society. I just had not quite got round to writing my little red book about it yet. In fact, Chairman Mao is still respected in China, as witnessed by the long queues developing in the early morning to visit his mausoleum in Tiananmen Square. They do accept he 'made a few mistakes', though – starting, perhaps, with the estimated one million mishaps resulting from the 'Great Leap Forward' and the Cultural Revolution. Actually, our Chinese tour guide rather bravely suggested that the people were queuing to see the embalmed body just to reassure themselves that Mao was dead. You will be reassured to know that there is truth in the adage that we drift to the right with age, education and wisdom, but since I started so far over to the left it is also little surprise that I have not quite met the midpoint in the political spectrum.

Next, faith. As a child, the world around me seemed to be consistently rational and full of wonder. I don't remember ever needing a belief in God to make sense of it. Clearly there were things I didn't know and things I would never know, but that didn't mean I had to fabricate an explanation to fill the void. To replace reason with conjecture and unsubstantiated dogma seemed a futile exercise. In my childhood innocence, I was even more suspicious of organised religion. I couldn't reconcile morning prayers which told me of religion's goodness, mercy and grace with the history textbooks in the afternoon describing its tendency towards violence and thirst for worldly wealth and political influence. Quite simply, I had no faith in the men of faith and I certainly didn't feel they had exclusive rights to set my moral compass. If I had any sense of God's presence, I might have had most sympathy with the Quakers' religious perspective. The lack of hierarchy and rituals, direct communion with their god, sympathy with scientific thought and a humanist approach to life all seem laudable, but I would be troubled by the pacifism. Without force, how else do you oppose tyranny? This would be a betrayal of all my father stood for and the thousands like him who paid a higher price for freedom. I had a brief sojourn in the Scouts, but despite identifying with Chippy in *The Wolf Patrol*, the mixture of childish militarism, lukewarm leftovers of empire and religious propaganda meant that my judo club won over the church parade in the Sunday-morning stakes. There was a final reassessment in the sixth form when we were obliged to receive some instruction on religious philosophy and I took pity on the kind and thoughtful religious education teacher. His penitence was to try to interest a bunch of adolescent free spirits in the Divine. I read some heavy tomes and delivered quite a good summary of the comparative perspectives of science and religion, but the die was cast.

One of Philip Larkin's most famous and iconic lines would have relevance when it came to sex. Except that it was nearer 1971! The whole area of human relationships was never discussed at home. Mum was quite prudish and would tut-tut if a couple entered anything more than a chaste embrace on the television. I never received any manly advice or instruction from my father. It was a more innocent time and knowledge of the act was very vague, as befits the sex education I received from poorly informed classmates, their confident pronouncements based on speculation and half-truths from older siblings. I never had any question about which way the wind was blowing, however, as borne testimony by my puerile interest in the glamour models beginning to appear in the red tops. But the combination of a single-sex secondary school and sublimation in sport and bookwork meant that I was a late developer.

Finally, in Nottingham I came to my own conclusion that, as often quoted by agony aunts, girls are not alien species and could safely be removed from the pedestal. Have fun, treat them with respect like you would any other friend and let nature take its course. I stopped looking with unrequited yearning at unattainable Julie Christie lookalikes with flowers in their hair dancing at the front of discos and began meeting *people*. They just happened to be the opposite sex, that's all. I met Jane and we had a totally chaste relationship, tripping out in the car to beauty spots around the Nottingham countryside, chatting away like an old couple. I never had any romantic leanings and not once did I detect any from my female friend, but we had a good time and I enjoyed her company. This must sound so old-fashioned to those used to swiping iPhones to find potential mates or passing ships in the night, but the echoes of '50s puritanism were still resonating.

"If I only knew then what I know now." How often do we hear that? In much later years I would sometimes stand at the front of a lecture theatre and, with an objective and fatherly eye, look at the sea of adolescent faces. Both male and female, they were all, without exception, attractive young men and women. True, some had minor imperfections in one way or another – the odd crook in the nose, flyaway hair, a pointed chin or slightly sticky-out ears – but they were all gorgeous-looking. And the reason was their youth and vitality; the teenage glow radiating and transcending all other physical characteristics. How much time must many of them have wasted in front of the mirror, fretting about a minor flaw when they held all the aces if only they had known it? If you are a baby boomer and don't believe me, just dig out that yellow, faded photo from your youth in the '60s.

As I watched the students in animated chatter before my lecture began, it was not just their youthful appearance that impressed. Bright, receptive minds with their futures ahead of them, their energetic characters a force of nature as I was allowed a glimpse into their world. A world seen through fresh eyes, and yet to be jaded by the worries and responsibilities of adult life. Overheard fragments of conversation told me of their teenage preoccupations and, just for a moment, before I called them to order, I could hear the beautiful harmonies of *Forever Changes* drifting from a sunlit window.

6

A Genius or Two

It was a cold, black November night and I sat in the small glass shelter; alone in the single pool of light on the station platform. A viewer in a gallery might be wondering what this lonely character in an Edward Hopper picture was thinking and what backstory was hidden from view. My car was off the road and I was waiting for a train on Belmont Station on the Epsom Downs Line to take me back to my flat in Selhurst after a day at the Institute of Cancer Research, Sutton branch. Life had taken a quantum step and I was trying to adapt to the new surroundings, routines and colleagues.

I had moved to London and taken the flat with my former housemate from Nottingham, Alan. He was training to be an actuary and was working for an insurance company in Croydon. Selhurst was at that time a run-down area and the flat was damp, dark and dirty, but cheap. The landlord visited on rent days with his Alsatian dog and there was a suspicious character in the basement who was forever carrying television sets in and out. He may have been a repair man, but the arrival of several police cars one day put paid to that benefit of the doubt. The bath was in the kitchen under a worn Formica worktop and filled with the aid of a dilapidated gas boiler. I was woken one Saturday morning by a small explosion, shortly after which Alan appeared with face covered in soot and eyebrows singed, so it was showers in work from then on.

Lin had stayed in Nottingham for the year to study for a postgraduate certificate in education, but we tried to meet every three or four weeks. With my car back on the road, I would traverse London on a Friday night to reach the M1. Driving alone and in the absence of satnavs, I zigzagged my way across the city with an internal compass pointing roughly north until I reached the motorway. Still, it was not like driving to Denmark!

I suspect that leaving the closeted life of university and joining the real world is a traumatic event for many young people. Certainly, I found it so and I don't think I was an easy person to live with over the course of the year. It was my first realisation that, while change is almost always positive in the longer term, it can also be painful in the short. The flat in Selhurst was also a useful reminder that poor living conditions and little money can make life very miserable. For me, at least, there were prospects of social and financial progress in the future.

Uncle Joe threw back his head and laughed long and hard. He had just removed the distributor from my ancient Hillman Minx and the contents, consisting of springs, weights, points and assorted other components, fell in a heap on the ground. I had driven from Nottingham to Romford with an increasing cacophony of noise rattling beneath the bonnet and the cause was now self-evident. We cleaned the points, reassembled the distributor contents and set the spark gap with a feeler gauge. These days, with my car maintenance skills limited to filling the windscreen washer reservoir, I find it remarkable that I was once able to replace water pumps, starter motors and brake cylinders with confidence. My mentor was again Uncle Joe, who kept my old bangers on the road and taught me some basic mechanical skills.

Though my pride and joy, the Hillman had some serious mechanical flaws. There was no synchromesh between third and fourth gears, which meant that I had to double-declutch; a complex ballet on the pedals involving rapidly blipping the accelerator in neutral between gear changes. The car also rolled precariously, and with a bench front seat and no seatbelts, there was an alarming tendency to slide back and forth across the vehicle on cornering. The brakes were spongy and, by modern standards, the headlights were dim. Yet, with Joe's help, it served me well for work and leisure for two years.

A second Hillman Minx was less reliable. During a daily commute the temperature gauge showed overheating and steam appeared from under the bonnet. I drew to a halt on a busy shopping street in Croydon and saw that water was squirting from a hole in the radiator. In the days before I could afford roadside assistance, there was only one option – I set to work and removed the radiator, spied a red kiosk to phone a local supplier and headed off with the offending component on the bus. With a reconditioned radiator under my arm, I returned to the car to reassemble the cooling system. I was disconcerted, however, to find a police car parked behind mine and an officer gingerly examining my vehicle. I had left various tools under the car and, at the height of the Irish Republican Army (IRA) bombing campaign in 1974, the policeman was understandably suspicious. I was sensitive to his concerns. Indeed, a year or two later, Sir Gordon Hamilton Fairley, professor of medical oncology and former director of my own research institute, was killed inadvertently by an IRA car bomb as he left his home one morning. The officer eventually accepted my explanation and I continued with my repair. I had the good fortune of breaking down outside a florist and so a supply of water for the radiator was close to hand. Continuing my journey, I arrived in work just two hours late.

As usual, my wife was trouncing me as we watched *University Challenge*. I weakly proffered my standard defence strategy, namely, that the questions are consistently arts-biased, but I knew when

I was beaten. However, it set me thinking about the nature of intelligence. I certainly have problems with difficult crosswords, Mensa-like numerical puzzles and the ferociously difficult 'knights-move' reasoning required to win points on the television show *Only Connect*. I have needed to compensate by innate curiosity about the world, hard work and a stubborn drive to achieve any ambitions. Brilliant mathematicians and physicists, on the other hand, have near-savant numerical and problem-solving abilities, together with a level of imagination and creative conceptual thought which is denied to us mere mortals. A contrarian nature to swim against the tide of consensus thinking must also be valuable. One popular misconception is that university professors are, by definition, highly intelligent. I have indeed met some who are, but generally they are more akin to chief executives of major companies, with strong organisational skills, single-mindedness and a soupçon of charm and manipulative behaviour which can hover dangerously on the edge of psychopathy.

My PhD supervisor, Dr Nick Blackett, ran one of the research groups in the department of biophysics which was engaged in studying the growth and proliferation of primitive stem cells (or 'seed cells') in bone marrow. Long-limbed and preternaturally youthful, he was one of the brightest minds I encountered in my career but always seemed slightly out of phase with the real world, and frequent facial tics and mannerisms of speech did not help his cause. Nevertheless, he was a delightfully kind and gentle man, writing a beautiful letter to my daughter when she was born which welcomed her to the world and captured the essence of his character. Nick was not aided by being the son of one of the cleverest men of his generation – Professor Patrick Blackett (Baron Blackett), who was an experimental and theoretical physicist who worked with Rutherford in the Cavendish Laboratory at Cambridge. I would recommend readers explore the achievements of this outstanding man in more detail, but briefly, his work using the cloud chamber led to fundamental discoveries in particle physics, confirming the existence of the positron and developing the concept of antimatter. As a sideline, he developed an interest in geophysics and helped find strong evidence for continental drift. He was awarded the Nobel Prize for Physics in 1948, became president of the Royal Society in 1965, and was appointed to the Order of Merit in 1967.

It seemed that Nick, whose degrees were in physics, suppressed his natural instincts to become a pure physicist in order to assuage the sense of living in his father's shadow. To be fair, he also probably developed a career in cancer research to satisfy a deeply held social conscience. Certainly his father had strong left-wing tendencies and developed close links with colleagues and institutions in the Third World. Nevertheless, the result was that Nick would always be conflicted and never appeared completely at home in the 'soft' biological and medical sciences of the time. In a more recent era, he might have found fame and renown in the field of the Human Genome Project, where complex mathematical techniques and computer science are required to deal with the massive amounts of data generated by automated DNA-sequencing technology. Or in medical imaging and new techniques in radiology; another frontier area where physics and medical science closely overlapped.

If Nick was a physicist uncomfortable in a field of medical science, I gradually came to the opinion that I was in the opposite situation. With a bias towards medical physics and mathematics, the department had made its name in cytokinetics, which concerns the measurement of the rate of cell division, tissue growth and proliferation in normal and tumour tissues. One of the notable advances was to recognise that cancers grow not because the cells divide more rapidly, but because they fail to die. Cell biology and biochemistry were later to identify the precise mechanisms of this failure of cell death. I studied the properties of the primitive stem cells in bone marrow and how they respond to damage by anti-cancer drugs. It was critical information needed to transform, for example, bone marrow transplantation for leukaemia patients from theory to reality. However, my biological approach and training were at odds with the numerical ethos of the department and I never felt completely at ease.

The field of cytokinetics had probably reached its zenith by the time I joined the laboratory. As in most things, a certain amount of luck is involved in being in the right place at the right time and science is no different. This was best exemplified by a colleague of mine who came to work in a research laboratory I was attached to in the '80s. During this period, genetic research underwent a revolution when a number of elegant techniques became available to analyse DNA. The polymerase chain reaction (PCR) is a remarkably simple method for amplifying a short section of DNA so that a few molecules are replicated to form many millions of identical copies. The product can be identified as a distinct fluorescent band after loading on a horizontal agarose gel and applying a charge gradient. This will be familiar to anybody who enjoys watching forensic science dramas, and the technique also allows specific defects (mutations) in the DNA of patients with genetic diseases to be identified with ease.

The PCR technique, which furnished a Nobel Prize for Kary Mullis in 1993, involves three chemical sequences which are temperature-dependent, and my colleague sat at the bench with three water baths and three stopwatches to perform the repetitive cycles by hand. Transferring tubes from one water bath to the next forty times, the whole process took around three hours and was exhausting, unreliable and time-consuming. Triumphantly, at the end of the six-month project he had a number of photographs of gels showing DNA bands. A couple of weeks after he had finished, however, the first commercial rapid DNA cyclers became available. In no time, his approach had been entirely superseded by new automated technology which could be safely left to do all the laborious work overnight.

While I was there, this laboratory was at the height of its powers and was led by some extremely dynamic and gifted scientists.

Scientific papers in prestigious journals flowed from our group and I was very fortunate to be part of it. On one occasion, we were studying a patient with a rare, severe form of the inherited bleeding disorder known as von Willebrand disease. We knew that one of fifty-two possible sections of DNA in his gene was missing, which accounted for the complete absence of the clotting factor in his blood. After a Herculean amount of work by my colleagues, the answer was found. We might as well have saved all the effort, though, and listened to Deep Thought in Douglas Adams' *The Hitchhiker's Guide to the Galaxy*. You have guessed it – the answer was forty-two! Of course, these days an automated DNA sequencer could provide the answer in an hour or two.

At the end of the year, life improved. Lin came down to London and managed to secure a post teaching history at Westwood School in Welling. We found a lovely, but tiny, wooden cottage in Hayes, Kent for a very reasonable rent. The cottage was semi-detached and the elderly lady who owned it lived alongside. To comply with the social mores of the time, we allowed her to assume that we were married. This sometimes required nimble footwork in conversation, and even more so when we decided to arrange our wedding for the October. It was a small ceremony in a Romford Registry Office with just parents; my grandmother, Alice; other close family and a few university friends. We fashioned a tissue of untruths to explain our unusually smart appearance on the morning of the event and buttonholes needed to be put in later.

Lin and I agreed on a simple civil ceremony, but it was clear that this was not well received by my mother. Secretly she would have expected a white wedding in a local church with all the trimmings. My mother had a complex personality and our relationship was no less complicated. When she was young, Betty was full of fun and good humour. Aunt Dorothy describes a teenager full of the joys of life and keen on dancing and going out with boys. Nevertheless, she had strong moral values and, once married, would always put her husband's and family's needs before her own. She carried both physical and emotional scars from her younger life, but there was still a lot of laughter in our childhood. I remember her almost wetting herself between uncontrollable bouts of giggling and hyperventilation when we played blow football on the living-room table one day. Despite the modest household income, she was generous and scrupulously even-handed to us children, never giving to one without the other. When I was seventeen, she decided that learning to drive was an important asset and somehow found the twenty-two shillings and sixpence for each of my eighteen lessons. And she didn't complain when I failed the first test and she had to find the money for a further six. Nor did I receive the scolding I expected when, kicking a ball outside Dorothy and Joe's caravan one day, one of my new school shoes flew off and, followed by several sets of disbelieving eyes, soared and arced in slow motion before disappearing below the surface of the adjacent moat. 'Boys will be boys' was all very well, but the cost of footwear must have severely tested her sense of forgiveness. Mum ensured I had a quality tennis racket to take to the Wimbledon tournament and, as I only had one set of tennis clothes, she dutifully washed and ironed them dry each night as we unexpectedly progressed through the week.

She also gave rare hints of a gentler nature buried beneath the brittle protective surface. I described a minor disagreement with Lin before we were married, and my mother was vexed. "You shouldn't let the wind blow on her," she said softly, which I thought was such sweet and poetic advice.

With our temperaments more similar than I would like to admit, our relationship became tenser in my late teenage years. My adolescent cheek and lawyer's way with words provided the charcoal and my mother's short fuse and inflexibility served as the sulphur. A relatively minor disagreement could add the saltpetre and the explosive cocktail was primed to blow. I recall a particularly acrimonious argument over the parental contribution to my university keep which left an acrid smell of spent gunpowder in the house for several days. My parents were unable to find the money and, indeed, were probably unaware of this admittedly vague concept. And I did not expect to receive it. However, my mother was looking for some gratitude for providing my living expenses during the Easter vacation when I didn't work, and I argued that it was compensation for their lack of contribution to my grant. Cue intractable positions and rising voices. A few emollient words from either side would have defused the situation, but it was not in either of our natures to avoid a conflict with such an easy solution. On another occasion, I accused my mother of 'verbal diarrhoea' and received a rare thump from my father which, grudgingly and with the passage of time, I suppose I deserved.

When my parents were first married, they lived for a short time in a prefab in Romford. Constructed soon after the war as a short-term fix for the housing shortage, they served the pressing need so well that many inhabitants were resistant to moving out and ended up staying for many decades. There are a handful remaining in Bristol and London and small numbers have been preserved with Grade II listed status. My parents' memory of sitting on deckchairs around orange boxes for a table mirrored our fond thoughts of Lin learning to cook for a dinner party in our small cottage on a Baby Belling. Very likely the nostalgia was as much about the exuberance of newlyweds and the promise of a shared life together as the basic accommodation.

For the remainder of our time in Kent, we lived a settled existence of domesticity and continued the process of fully getting to know each other. With Lin earning and my small grant, we felt slightly more solvent and managed a few trips to theatres and an occasional restaurant meal. At weekends we visited local historic sites and beauty spots including the magnificent first-century Roman villa and mosaic at Lullingstone, and the adjacent picturesque village of Eynsford. We lacked a picnic set and so Lin pre-prepared full plates of salad, put them on the back seat of the Hillman and we headed off to Sissinghurst Castle Garden for a leisurely stroll in Vita Sackville-West and Harold Nicolson's peaceful creation. Investing in a small tent from Kays catalogue, and with the impulsiveness of youth, we sometimes decided to set off after supper on a Friday evening to drive down the A21 towards Camber Sands and camp on the Sussex coast.

In time, I made good friends in the department. James, a fellow researcher, invited us to his rather grand flat in Chelsea and it was difficult to think that we had navigated similar routes to reach this transient meeting place in our lives. He clearly functioned in a more rarified social sphere, but he was kind and supportive as I found my feet in the new academic environment. At lunchtimes, I played tennis with another postdoctoral scientist, Chris, and a visiting professor from Canada joined us for a game one day. He was fun, friendly and approachable. It was only sometime later that I realised I had had the honour of playing with Professor Harold Johns – a famous medical physicist who developed the so-called 'Cobalt bomb', a pioneering machine which allowed safe, calibrated doses of gamma radiation from a Cobalt-60 source to be used to treat cancer. Sam was another Canadian and a fellow PhD student in the department. He was something of an exception for a man of those parts, with challenging opinions and a mildly assertive manner, but he was an engaging companion and became a good friend before returning to Canada for a successful career in the pharmaceutical industry.

Our cottage was a stone's throw from Down House, the former home of Sir Charles Darwin, but ancient echoes of his learning were failing to convince me that my future lay primarily in the research laboratory. The urge to study medicine where science was applied in a social context had continued to simmer in my mind, but this time I had somebody by my side who was sympathetic and encouraging. Lin's selfless attitude was, "If you really want to do it, carry on and I will support you emotionally and financially." I still hesitated, but it was on a knife edge. The balance was tipped by a throwaway line from an elderly man who ran the local football team I played for in Welling. Giving him a lift back home after a match one day, I treated him to a monologue on my dilemma.

After a thoughtful pause, and with the wisdom of age, he quietly ventured, "Well, if you are not doing one thing, you are doing another."

I'm still not sure whether this comment was deeply banal or deeply profound, but at the time it felt like an epiphany. Of course! Why didn't I think of that – if I'm not doing one thing, I'm doing another.

And so that was it. I requested a university admissions form, sent off the application with the new Nottingham Medical School as my first preference, and sat back with a mixture of relief and nervous anticipation. Now all I had to do was complete the PhD and hopefully embrace the new beginning. Well, it was a little more complicated than that. If I was successful, it would be a further five years of study. In more recent times, abbreviated medical courses for science graduates have been established, but these were not available in the UK at the time. I looked very seriously at McMaster Medical School in Canada, which did offer a three-year course of this type, and even filled in application forms, but the practicalities seemed insoluble. It was another of life's crossroads and, in one of the infinite number of multiverses my wife and I exist in, we might be wealthy Canadians with a house overlooking Lake Ontario and spending weekends fishing in the Great Lakes with my friend, Sam. As the famous philosopher Jean-Paul Sartre once said, *We are our choices.*

We anticipated that at the forthcoming interview, there would be less emphasis on academic achievement and more on how I was going to support myself for five years. This proved correct and I had to demonstrate that we had given this some thought. My wife, of course, was working and had vowed to support us both. We had saved a modest sum of money and we had parents who had promised to help if they could. With projected optimism but inner pessimism, I also added, "And I have applied for another local authority grant." This must have been sufficient because I was given an unconditional offer.

Some weeks later, my wife and I were stunned when we opened the letter from the Havering Education Department. I had been awarded a full grant for the whole five years! This was exceptional even in those times. Romford, with a Labour-controlled council, had truly come up trumps for an old boy and I wrote them an effusively grateful letter – and in the future, thanked them again when their investment had borne fruit. This is difficult to write now, knowing that present-day students have a yoke of major debt around their neck for a lifetime, but what can I say? These were more enlightened times when only a few decades before, the austerity of post-war Britain and the penury of national war debts somehow failed to prevent the flowering of the welfare state and the NHS. With the aid of my sister doing the typing, and a quietly knitting wife, I sat down to write my PhD, which was an eight-month slog. To be honest, it was not a brilliant piece of work; more a cliché of perspiration over inspiration. Again, however, it was a means to an end. It was completed a few weeks before returning to Nottingham and, after a successful viva, we headed off again into the light and the open road.

7

A New Beginning – Again

I couldn't breathe. I couldn't breathe, and I had to get out! I couldn't breathe, I had to get out, and I had to run, anywhere! The rising panic transfixed me in the lecture theatre and, in the manner of a near-death experience, I was on the outside of my mind and body, looking in. The lecturer, a renowned Home Office pathologist, continued his trawl through a personal slide collection of murders, violent deaths and fatal accidents, but I had to leave. With the suddenness of the train hitting the head of the man who had inadvisably leaned a little too far out of the carriage window, I had crashed into a full-blown anxiety attack. The past year had caught up with me and my subconscious had dispatched a warning; the inner self does not have unlimited capacity for stress and the eight months of obsessive behaviour at the table in Hayes did not come without payback.

Over the following six months I experienced the full spectrum of neurotic symptoms: free-floating anxiety, depersonalisation, unwelcome and frightening obsessive thoughts, and a variety of physical symptoms which, if I hadn't a modicum of medical knowledge, I would have interpreted as the onset of a fatal illness. I suffered claustrophobia; the main shopping centre in

Nottingham was notorious for its low ceilings and dim lighting and was impossible for me to enter. Lectures were a trial; would I cry, shout or laugh inappropriately? In reality there was no chance that I would, but the possibility stoked my sense of panic. This was a horrible experience, and don't let any doubting Thomas tell you that this is a trivial illness. They quite clearly have never suffered the condition. I sought a sympathetic ear at the student health centre and a few Valium were forthcoming which were of doubtful benefit. Though my wife may have had suspicions, I largely kept the inner turmoil to myself. One big positive was that I did not have any symptoms of depression, which might have been even more debilitating and have had greater impact on my life and studies. I never sunk into hopelessness or torpor and, in fact, remained confident throughout that time would be the great healer. And so it was. The painful episode, however, left me with a hard-earned and profound empathy for patients with affective disorders.

In retrospect, other factors apart from feeling emotionally drained after writing up the PhD were causing me concern. I had a fear of the stigma of being labelled a perpetual student, and also a sense that perhaps all my efforts on the previous degrees had been wasted. A return to a life of lectures and exams was discombobulating and I had to adapt to the role of being a highly qualified and more mature figure in a class which was six or seven years younger than I. In reality, and as time would prove, none of these concerns would hold up to scrutiny, and were simply the irrational fears of a damaged young mind.

In fact, there were four other mature students on the course, which was somewhat innovative for medical schools at that time: a chap with a PhD in physics, and two graduates with degrees in biochemistry and metallurgy, respectively. There was also Mary, who was even more mature and loved by all. She would later become a well-respected general practitioner and die too soon – but her presence remains at our reunions, which continue to this day.

Gradually, the negative feelings provoked by overwork and the abrupt change in my personal status and direction subsided and were replaced by a strong sense of privilege and gratitude. With Lin's help, I had achieved a long-held dream to enter medical school and I set to work with renewed vigour to make the best of my good fortune.

The medical course was composed of two and a half years of preclinical work, mainly lectures, practicals and demonstrations, followed by a similar period of clinical attachments in different sub-specialties, for example, general medicine and surgery, obstetrics and gynaecology, dermatology etc. The small year of forty-eight medical students soon became a tight-knit group; bonds which would only increase over the years as we shared all the intense experiences of our early forays into an exciting new world. As expected, in many subjects – biochemistry, pharmacology and physiology, for example – I had good foundations. Anatomy was, however, new, and the factual detail daunting.

There was an air of nervous anticipation laced with an odour of formalin when we were introduced to our cadavers lying under white sheets on their dissection tables. The male corpse was later to be christened Mabel, but was otherwise treated with the utmost respect. In a group of six, five of us tentatively moved forward to nervously view the body when the drapes were removed. The sixth, my great friend, Graham, immediately dived in to explore his natural territory and couldn't wait to put scalpel to skin. Soon, he would leave us in his wake as he followed every nerve, examined the course of every blood vessel and, with mounting enthusiasm, documented the attachments of every muscle. He rapidly memorised the eight bones in the wrist and the names of all the entry and exit holes in the skull (foramina, to the experts!).

Graham was demonstrating a well-recognised phenomenon which would only be obvious in retrospect. Our personalities and interests were, even at this early stage, beginning to show leaning towards our eventual career specialties. And you would have no problem anticipating Graham's path – he was always going to be a general surgeon. The quiet and thoughtful with a pronounced caring side became general practitioners (GPs), the slightly eccentric became psychiatrists or pathologists, the rugby players became orthopaedic surgeons, and the self-confident, hands-on types became anaesthetists. I exaggerate a little, but there was a hint of truth in these stereotypes. I have kept some of my old medical books in the loft, and the yellowing, loose-bound anatomy primers still carry the odour of formalin as a powerful reminder of those wonderful days.

Both Graham and I had a problem with public health. To a prospective surgeon and a scientist, it was a 'soft' science lacking the sharpness and clarity of our chosen fields. After receiving the results of the only exam he was ever to fail, Graham was indignant that the perfect answers he provided failed to receive due credit. He was totally unpersuaded that the carefully crafted responses bore absolutely no relation to the questions on the paper! This single blot on an otherwise shining career would later become a badge of honour.

We were asked to split into small groups and plan a project. On hearing that a nearby factory in Beeston was about to close, we decided to measure anxiety scores with questionnaires. Where did that idea come from, I wonder? With my added experience we produced quite a polished piece of work. In the viva, however, the lecturer, who had a rather forceful personality, chose to ignore our efforts and I was asked repeatedly about the difference between incidence and prevalence. I became increasingly sullen until he began pointing at me with his pencil, whereupon a small explosion occurred. I passed the exam, but was to join Graham on the epidemiologist's naughty step.

The noise was deafening, the hot air thick with dust, and there was an acrid smell of smoke and molten metal in the atmosphere. A huge bucket of orange-yellow liquid, radiating heat and light, swung from the roof in an otherwise black void. Massive metal rolling machines, giant coke hoppers and occasional blackened figures dwarfed in the shadows completed the Dantean scene. We were on a trip to Stanton and Staveley Steelworks in Ilkeston to learn about the role of occupational health physicians in the industry. It was one of a number of visits which had the added bonus of giving some of my younger and perhaps more sheltered colleagues insight into the working lives of ordinary people. Of course, I gained my early experience of manual labour and a hazardous workplace in the bubblegum factory. The plant closed in 2007, so more recent students will have been unable to share our good fortune in having this memorable experience.

We also visited Rampton Secure Hospital in the north of Nottinghamshire, which housed some of the most dangerous psychiatric patients in the country. Though built in 1912, there were echoes of the Victorian both in the buildings and the ethos. No doubt things have changed over the past forty years, but it surprised me then that the hospital staff lived in a self-contained community within its walls; an incarcerated village reminiscent of Portmeirion transformed for the fictional series *The Prisoner*. My memory is hazy, but I believe there were seven levels of security, and our trepidation increased as we approached the highest. A group of patients were located in a square room at the centre, with a continuous corridor running round the four sides and windows for observation. An inner sanctum of profound evil or sad psychopathology, depending on your point of view. Pairs of staff were located at each corner and always had to be visible to two sets of colleagues. We were told that some of the patients were too dangerous to have direct contact with, and that it was advisable for staff to avoid entering their personal space.

Another visit we were privileged to make was to a working coal mine. We were not to know that this was living history and that the mining industry, and many of the Nottingham communities supporting it, would be obliterated over the following decade or two. Covered in grime and in the half-light, we crept along the coalface on hands and knees as the metal supports creaked and groaned around us. At the end, in the gloom, a miner sat eating his sandwiches. He described how a six-foot guardsman on a similar visit froze halfway along and could barely be persuaded to move in either direction.

I had a friend in Nottingham who was vacating a flat just off Mansfield Road. Before moving up from London, Lin and I decided to visit it and, wanting to save every penny, camped at a site in Cropwell Bishop, a village to the east of the city. On arrival, we found the site flat with good facilities, but yin is always balanced by yang; the yang in this case being interminable pit trains passing on the adjacent railway at 4am. It formed a base, however, and we took off to visit the flat. Well, it was a step up from Selhurst – but not by much. Nevertheless, it would do until we found something better. As luck would have it, we bought a local newspaper and our curiosity was pricked when we noted the house prices. The East Midlands has always been behind the curve, and we saw modest houses we thought we might afford. The following day, with only our rough camping clothes available, we entered a local Halifax Building Society branch dressed like hobos who had hopped off a passing pit train. To our surprise, they agreed to advance us a mortgage and that was how, in 1974, we bought a small, three-bed terraced new build for the princely sum of £6,200.

From the front window of our new house, we watched the kitten walk nervously along the first-floor windowsill before dropping to the ground. My wife and I rushed over and found her meowing but without injury. A beautiful grey bundle of fluff, we immediately fell in love with her and took her back to our house for milk and chicken scraps. Later that day we despondently returned the kitten to her owner, but destiny was again to take a hand. The neighbour called back a few days later to say they were moving and would we like to keep her? There was never any doubt, and so began an eighteen-year relationship with a special friend: Pussy Willow.

Though not a pure breed, she had many characteristics of a Russian Blue. Despite her small size, she was fearless and soon took her place at the head of the household. It has been said that she had the imperial pretensions of a feline tsarina mixed with the aggressive instincts of a wildcat. However, she could be loving and loyal; waiting all day beneath a shed at the end of the road to await my wife's return from work late in the afternoon. With a maternal eye and retracted claws, she would perch on the back of the settee and idly bop any passing two-year-old on the top of the head – much to the surprise of the exclaiming recipient. On the other hand, the vet also labelled her "the most aggressive cat [he had] encountered" as, with her hissing and snarling, he tentatively removed clamped claws from around his arm. On another occasion, she dragged a dead leveret through a skylight window and presented it to us proudly.

She seemed unable to avoid being the centre of attention. A close friend visited us in Nottingham to unburden his concerns about the sad state of his marriage. We listened quietly and sympathetically as the conversation became increasingly emotional. At this critical moment, Pussy Willow strode into the room, surveyed her domain – and nonchalantly dropped a live field mouse from her jaws into the centre of the carpet. For a second or two, we sat speechless and open-mouthed, as the shared empathy of the moment was lost forever. Then, as the mouse ran across the room, up the curtain and perched on the rail, all semblance of order dissolved. The three of us chased the rodent around the room before finally trapping it in a towel. Meanwhile, Pussy Willow sat with a detached air, busying herself with personal hygiene. Then with a final glance at the chaos she had achieved, she wandered out of the door – mission accomplished!

Our cat lived a good life and, in her later years, had the benefit of a safe home in the country for her wanderings. She struck up a platonic friendship with a large ginger tom and, age having tempered her belligerence, they wandered in the local woods together in elderly companionship. As she became increasingly frail, we put her in a cattery for one final break, but she died before we returned from holiday. The owner, knowing that she was a well-loved pet, kindly kept her in the cattery deep freeze before helping my grieving wife bury her beneath the bronze beech at the end of our garden. We sometimes catch a glimpse of her up there; green eyes flashing and grey tail swishing in the shadows, as she goes about her business in the moonlight.

With my wife working at a close-by school and new friends on the course, our social life was not wanting. In particular, our small house became a refuge for student friends who wanted to escape the campus, or who had moved a little more rapidly into maturity and wished to have respite from the high jinks of hall life. I later met a chap originally from the Middle East, a young scientist who became a close friend. Intelligent and perceptive, he gave us reflections on the UK which were only obvious to someone born elsewhere. As I remember, his father had close links with the British Embassy at home and permission was given for him to come to England for school and university. When he visited our house, he gave us interesting perspectives on Middle Eastern politics and was proud of his culture and close family. We learnt much about the former and cemented our friendship by meeting many of his kin, including his father and younger brothers.

One day, without thinking too intently about my question, I asked our new friend whether he was affected by the Six Day War in 1967 between Israel and Egypt, Syria and Jordan. Gently replying in a way that didn't repay me for my blundering crassness, he said that he had lost several very close relatives during the conflict. We persuaded him to buy a small tent and went off camping together in Snowdonia and along the North Norfolk coast. It was an alien concept in his homeland, and he had great fun embracing the freedom of weekends under canvas. On one occasion, however, I asked him to find a rock to deal with an intransigent tent peg and he looked nervous and uncertain. He knew very well that lifting rocks in the English countryside was safe, but a childhood fear of finding a lurking scorpion had not fully left him.

As I continued on the medical course, the déjà vu of revisiting familiar science subjects in the first year or two was not as tedious as I anticipated. It was a relief, however, when, after two years, we were allowed to choose a specialist area for a project and deeper enquiry. I chose pathology as a relevant topic which I had little knowledge of. Before commencing, I was surprised when a consultant with an interest in blood cancers contacted me. John Fletcher had heard that I had a background in leukaemia research and offered me the opportunity to join his small team for my third-year project. The study of stem cells in humans was now possible since it had been shown that they could be grown on a plate of warm agar jelly in the laboratory. They could also be detected in the blood, which made them easy to access. The 'right place, right time' principle worked in my favour and I had fun setting up the technique, which provided plenty of data. However, I needed a novel twist to finish. I had read that patients with Down's syndrome and an extra chromosome 21 in their cells had an increased risk of leukaemia. Perhaps this was reflected in how their stem cells grew in the laboratory, and I formulated a plan to collect blood samples from some affected individuals. In the future, advanced molecular biology and genetic techniques would fully unravel this story which makes fascinating reading, but we are talking about forty years ago!

I contacted a number of residential homes and arranged to visit. At the first, the welcoming nurse introduced me to Billy. Middle-aged with little hair and a friendly grin, he remained resolutely mute but passively compliant as I gently took the sample and passed time chatting to the attractive young carer. Completing my task, I suddenly felt the urgency to return to the lab with the sample still fresh and I made a hurried goodbye to the nurse. I had walked ten steps when a voice stopped me in my tracks.

"Goodbye, Dr Standen," called Billy, in his first utterance.

I had done the unforgivable: Billy should have played a central role in the playlet and not been a minor character by the wings. I turned, hurried back and corrected my mistake, but the damage was done. Another lesson learned. Thankfully, the days of groups of doctors standing over their ignored patient and discussing his or her pathology amongst themselves should be long gone. If you ever visit an intensive care unit – and I hope you don't – watch how the nurses explain every action to their deeply unconscious patients, out of respect and in case of hidden awareness. I don't think I quite deserved my wife using this morality tale for years to come in her class assemblies, though.

My collaboration with John Fletcher was very fruitful and we published many papers together in well-read journals. This continued for the years I remained in Nottingham and I helped supervise a PhD student as I progressed through my medical degree. There was another interesting aspect to this story, however. At that time I was able to have an idea to research, and take the blood samples without a second thought. In retrospect, this was not acceptable and, rightly, there was a need for oversight, regulation and consent for any interventions involving patients. The failure to seek fully informed consent led to desperately sad scenarios like those described in the Bristol Heart Enquiry when samples and whole organs were taken from children post-mortem without their parents' permission and stored for future research. Needless to say, the parents were distressed and outraged by this oversight.

It has to be said that this was a grey area and accepted practice at the time, and I had sympathy with some of the excellent doctors who were caught on the wrong side of history – before ethics committees were established and new ethical codes developed which embraced transparency, communication and informed consent. Everybody would agree that this was a welcome development. However, the downside was that ethics committees soon became unwieldy and inefficient. There is a tendency for such committees to attract those who find it easier to think of a form rather than form a thought. Consequently, a totally laudable system became too bureaucratic and could often interfere with both research and teaching. In my early years as a consultant senior lecturer I took students in my research laboratory for six-month attachments. Usually, this would just involve using anonymised blood samples from the routine laboratory that would otherwise be discarded. Towards the end, however, the proliferation of forms and the lengthy delay of ethics approval meant that there was little time left to do the actual work, and I gave up the practice.

Nottingham Medical School produced its first young doctors in 1975 and Roger, my friend and trailblazer, was amongst them. In addition to the small size of the intake, the new school had a number of other benefits. The curriculum was designed to introduce some clinical components early in the course to whet the appetites of the students and give added motivation. The preclinical teachers were excited by the new lecture theatres and laboratories, and the pre-existing clinical staff from the old Nottingham hospitals were uniformly enthusiastic and stimulated by their new status as teaching hospital consultants. There was a definite buzz around the place.

We were lucky – our small intake meant that, when the time came to be attached to clinical firms, individual tuition was often the order of the day. In my later years working in an old established teaching hospital, there were in excess of two hundred students in each year and large groups were barely manageable on the wards for clinical teaching. Personalised and individual teaching on our course was particularly relevant when it came to learning practical skills. Most students were keen to learn how to perform a lumbar puncture in patients with suspected meningitis, aspirate fluid from around the lungs of smokers breathless with lung cancer, or insert urinary catheters in patients whose passage of urine from the bladder had become obstructed. We were fortunate in having little competition on the ward amongst our peers and, once we had nagged the house officer to take us through the procedure, another skill could be added to the tally. Practical procedures also provided a sharp reminder of why we had to learn all that detail in the anatomy class. At 4am when you were about to plunge a wide-bore needle into the chest of a patient unable to breathe because of a large pleural effusion, it suddenly became very relevant to know the path of the intercostal artery and vein as they run between the ribs! In obstetrics, we were obliged to attend and assist at the delivery of fifteen babies. This was a magical experience and one of my most treasured memories of medical training. On call in the first week, the complement of midwives seemed to take a shine to me and rushed me from room to room around the labour suite. Seven mums would have my name against theirs in the medical notes that night.

Another teaching innovation in Nottingham which was later more widely adopted involved the use of video to record the interactions between students and actors or actresses playing mock patients. Susan was first up, and introduced herself in a professional manner to the young woman slouching in the chair opposite.

"Tell me, what's the problem?" she enquired.

"I've got a tapeworm, I think," came the unexpected and wrong-footing reply.

We could see Susan swallow and sit back in her chair, playing for time as she marshalled her thoughts. She knew as much about tapeworms as I did, which was nothing. However, undeterred, she leaned in and began to expertly tease out the real reason for the girl's visit. How her boyfriend had recently dumped her and the hint of abuse in her childhood; the grumbling tummy ache and the thought that she might be pregnant. At the end, the actress was in floods of false tears and our eyes were glistening with real ones. We all gave them a clap.

Next up was Peter. With his strong northern accent and generally calm demeanour, he introduced himself.

"So good of you to find the time to see me," came the sarcastic reply.

As he asked sensible questions about the nature of the actor's problems, the answers became increasingly confrontational. Peter, who up to now had stayed calm, began to bristle. The actor recognised his chance, raised the stakes and began a tirade of criticism against the NHS.

By this time, Pete had lost it. He was no longer in the lecture theatre, role-playing with an actor. He was in the real world, struggling to contain his anger. And then the dam burst. He stood up, banged his hands on the table and, raising his voice, uttered the immortal words: "Now let me tell you, we have got some of the finest doctors in the world in Britain and you are lucky to have them!"

The teacher pressed the buzzer before the confrontation turned physical!

What impressed me most was the craft of the young actors and actresses, who must have been from a local stage school. The awkward characters they portrayed were sometimes not far removed from the truth, however. Many years later, I welcomed a married couple into my consulting room and offered them a seat. As I began discussing the woman's symptoms, the husband butted in to give his opinions and gradually became increasingly rude and difficult. I carried on and took a piece of paper to draw a picture explaining the mechanism of his wife's pernicious anaemia. At this point, the husband grabbed the sheet, screwed it up and threw it across the room. I terminated the consultation and, bemused, said that I would phone her GP. When I did so a week later, I described the odd nature of the meeting.

"Oh, Bill," he replied. "He was sectioned at the weekend for a psychotic illness."

New experiences came thick and fast on the medical course as we traversed different attachments and specialties. We were learning to respect the privilege of being invited into patients' lives when they were at their most vulnerable, both physically and emotionally. To show understanding, sympathy and empathy, but at the same time maintain an objective detachment so that our new medical knowledge and skills could be applied effectively. In accident and emergency (A&E), I sutured the head wound of a man attacked in the city centre; a six-inch slash across the scalp with the skull bone visible. He was dressed in a gold lurex top and tight black skirt, and his running mascara accentuated the sadness in his eyes. To encourage a holistic view, we were encouraged to ask patients clerked on the medical ward whether we might visit them at home after recovery. The pale, jaundiced lady with haemolytic anaemia who was too weak to rise from her bed looked very different as I sat sipping from her dainty bone china teacup in her immaculate sitting room. Matching the riot of floral design, her rosy cheeks told me the steroids prescribed had arrested the self-destruction of her red cells and her full face and second piece of Battenberg implied that she was still taking the medication – which induces a voracious appetite. On a GP attachment I spent a morning with a quadriplegic patient; a young man anchored in a dim bungalow bedroom since one last fateful ride on his motorcycle. Carers visited every few hours, but he was pleased to see a different face and tell his story to someone new. With the GP I visited an old man at home in one of the last remaining areas of Nottingham slum housing, most of which had been demolished in the early 1970s. He was sitting in a small kitchen surrounded by dirt, squalor and mildew, with filthy linoleum on the floor. The practice of medicine in this environment was very different to the hospital experience where the full range of diagnostic resources were available. Watching my mentor apply his craft in such a setting would sustain my respect for GP colleagues working in the community for the rest of my career.

The new Nottingham Medical School was a brand leader in another aspect of medical education. There were equal numbers of male and female students on our course. In part, this was driven by the zeitgeist of gender politics at the time, but also because young women were simply more mature than their male counterparts and could apply themselves to work for the high A Level grades required. Women could no longer be ignored.

Because the female consultants of that era had had to penetrate an arcane, male-dominated profession in the '50s, they had to have exceptional qualities. It also meant they could be quite intimidating. Even approaching the age of thirty and with my clutch of degrees, the surgeon, Miss P, could make me quake as a student. She was a spare, bespectacled woman with a precise manner of speech and a penetrating gaze.

"And the features of Hirschsprung's disease are...?

"And you would manage this patient with pyloric stenosis how?"

Later, one Sunday morning as I worked as a junior houseman on the medical ward, a new admission arrived. It was Miss P, and I took a step back, caught between my new-found professional confidence and my student subservience. She was due to have routine investigations for a minor problem and was booked to stay for a day or two. Stripped of her professional veneer, she was delightful and we hit it off immediately. We went to the restroom, chatted like old friends, and I showed her a blackbird's nest full of young which I had spotted in the gutter of an adjacent ward block. Later, just visible over the steering wheel of her powerful Saab, she would visit us for afternoon tea and we remained friends until we left Nottingham.

Miss M was an obstetrician with the glamour of a film star, who also taught me as a student. She took it in good part when the Medics football team made her president of the club. We were invited round for wine and cheese at her upmarket apartment in a classy area of the city. I remember us all trooping in to be met by an endless vista of apparently brand-new, pure-white carpet. I could not relax at any point in the evening as I watched every glass of precariously balanced red wine hover over the arctic pile.

One of the demonstrators helping us to make sense of the complexities of the human body in the anatomy class was a young surgeon, Angus Wallace. He would go on to become professor of orthopaedics in the medical school, and gained fame in 1995 when, on a flight from Hong Kong to London, he improvised rudimentary surgical equipment to treat a woman who had a tension pneumothorax. This potentially fatal condition develops when the lung is punctured and air builds up in the pleural cavity, eventually leading to cardio-respiratory failure. I remember a very old man being admitted with this condition one day when I was a houseman. He was in extremis, not far from cardiac arrest, and I had a dilemma. Without time to arrange an X-ray, I could rely on my clinical skills, hope my diagnosis was correct and immediately plunge a chest drain between his ribs – or not. Fortunately, I chose active intervention, and there was a reassuring escape of trapped air before his breaths became slower and deeper and he rallied.

Orthopaedic surgeons are well known for their self-confidence and self-belief. I once went to an education centre in Abergavenny which, on the same afternoon, had inadvisably booked a group of orthopaedic surgeons on a management course and a group of public service workers for assertiveness training. The surgeons thought it great fun to steal all the cakes from the civil servants' table set for tea. Having been offered a mean plate of digestive biscuits in their own room, they were not about to allow the meek to inherit the Danish pastries in the other. I rather suspect they were playing to the stereotype, though.

Whilst Angus' heroics were at the extreme end of the spectrum, it is not unusual for doctors on aeroplanes to be asked to identify themselves to treat in-flight medical emergencies. Most will keep their head down and hope that a colleague will attend. As a reward for my research efforts, John Fletcher offered me the chance to go to Dallas for an experimental haematology meeting. It was my first flight and at about eight hours' duration, I accepted with some trepidation. All was going well until the call came:

"Is there a doctor on the plane? If so, please come to the forward cabin."

There was no response, which was extremely surprising given we were on a full jumbo jet flying to the States. As a junior doctor I did not feel too guilty continuing to read my magazine. When the call came a second time, and then a third, however, I felt obliged to leave my seat and venture forward. A less naive soul would have had serious reservations as it was a Braniff Airways flight and the American legal system would take no account of the 'Good Samaritan' defence if something went wrong. The elderly lady had anxiety and faintness and, after a medical examination, I determined that nothing serious was going on. A flight attendant said that they could land in some icy wasteland if necessary but, unless there was a very good reason, there was no way I was going to put myself through another take-off and landing at this stage of my flying career.

Every so often, a politician will come up with the notion that pharmacists can act as inexpensive doctors; after all, they both know about drugs and their skills must be interchangeable. And, as has been said recently, "The British people have had enough of experts." Quietly, though, the professional bodies correct their misapprehensions. Pharmacists certainly do know a lot about drugs and they have a vital role in checking dosages, advising on side effects, looking out for drug interactions and much more. But medical prescribing is a whole different ball game, and this is the information taught in medical schools. First and foremost, it is important to have an in-depth clinical knowledge to be able to make an accurate diagnosis before prescribing.

Here is an example. An elderly lady visits a pharmacist because of backache and constipation. With a superficial assessment, he or she might advise a painkiller and a laxative. A doctor, however, might link the symptoms and wonder about the malignant bone marrow disorder myeloma, which often presents this way. The cancer cells destroy the bones of the spine, and increase the blood calcium which, in turn, causes constipation. The GP would have the ability and training to examine the patient to look for signs of vertebral collapse and nerve damage and know which simple tests to send off to exclude the diagnosis. 'Exclude' because in most cases the patient won't have myeloma – but you don't want to be the one who does who is dismissed by the pharmacist with paracetamol and senna! And if NHS England recommend that you take your child who may have meningitis but probably doesn't to a pharmacist, it may be worthwhile giving it a second thought. It is very unlikely that the pharmacist will have seen or examined a case of meningitis, and you would not wish your precious offspring to be their first attempt at this sometimes-challenging diagnosis.

This is no criticism of pharmacists who have an important role in the health service, and the relationship between the two professions is generally excellent. However, hands-on clinical expertise in diagnosis and therapeutics is not a core part of pharmacy training or practice and it is important that those outside health systems recognise that the specialties have very different skill sets.

8

And Then There Were Three

I was staying in London, and I phoned home to my parents to arrange a meetup. My mother answered, and in a quiet and slightly quivering voice said, "Your dad has been to the doctor today; his tummy is swollen and full of water."

There really is a sensation that the blood runs cold in moments like this; the cliché exists for a reason. My mind was racing with shock and abortive attempts to rationalise the news. I began running through my undergraduate's list of causes of ascites, the abnormal accumulation of watery tissue fluid in the abdominal cavity. There was no hiding place for hope; all of the possibilities were bad and most were dire. There was nothing to suggest Dad had chronic liver or kidney disease. I had seen a case of peritoneal tuberculosis, but that seemed very unlikely. It had to be malignancy, in which case, it was almost certainly terminal. I voiced a few non-committal words of comfort and arranged to see her alone in a coffee shop in Romford the following evening.

The irony was that I was spending the month in London on an elective at the Royal Marsden Hospital in South Kensington, one of the largest and most renowned cancer hospitals in the world. Electives were an opportunity to experience medicine in a totally different setting and many younger students showed enterprise; visiting the Third World or major centres of excellence in the States, Canada or Australia. I had a connection with the Marsden and the affiliated Institute of Cancer Research through my PhD. Oncology was a likely career path and, since Lin's teaching tied her to Nottingham, I decided to stay closer to home – which was fortunate. The experience at the Marsden would have been invaluable, but the month passed in a blur as I fought to process the grief, worry and concern for my father and the family. I was staying in a hospital house reputedly owned by Boris Karloff in the past, and the horror of the situation was entirely in keeping.

Being away from home was an ordeal but I had a saviour: my friend Peter was doing an elective in pathology at St Thomas'. In my hour of need he was supportive; a sympathetic sounding board as I unburdened my thoughts. It was 1977 and we went to see the first *Star Wars* film in Leicester Square, though I recall little apart from the opening sequence. We walked back through the London streets; me doing the talking, him attentive in his gentle, caring way.

My mother also had no hope. Weeks before, she had seen George standing in front of the mirror with swollen tummy and sagging muscles and knew that something was seriously wrong. In retrospect, he had looked tired and drawn for many months. She had seen too many relatives with malignancies to contemplate anything other than the worst possible outcome. Tearfully, we talked over some of the practicalities, planned how my brother and sister would be told and how we could possibly cope with the terrible journey we were about to embark on. From the outset, my mother was determined that George should not be told that he had a terminal illness. It was the only way, it was felt, that she and my sister living at home could cope with the situation. This denial was very difficult for me. My father was not an unintelligent man and the plan meant that a charade of avoidance and subterfuge had to be maintained. He would clearly know that he was dying, and it was against my medical and personal judgement that this was the correct path. But who was I to overrule Mum? I would be living in Nottingham, maintaining a semblance of a normal life between occasional visits, while they would be coping with the day-to-day slow and relentless decline of a much-loved husband and father. And so this approach was maintained until his death and I rarely had the opportunity to discuss his fears or his concerns for those he would be leaving.

There was one glimmer of light in the gloom which made an enormous difference to the family. George had an Indian friend at work, Fred, a gentle and gracious man who shared an interest in his union duties and clearly had the greatest respect and regard for my father. When he was too ill to work, Fred would visit each day, bring news of the office and perhaps allow my father to unburden concerns he could not share with his family. My mother continued to work in a department store for as long as possible and it was a great comfort that her precious husband could be safely left in the company of this good man who would remain dutifully by his side until the end.

George's illness was punctuated by visits to the hospital for removal of the accumulating fluid from his abdomen and, later, also from his chest. Examination of the samples showed cancer cells, but the type could not be identified. Though his abdomen was swelling, the rest of the physique of which he was so proud was gradually fading. Surprisingly, he remained fairly free of significant discomfort; I think it was beyond even my father to feign stoicism in the face of the pain of advancing cancer. I attempted to visit as often as possible, but my work was intensifying as I approached finals and I felt guilty for not doing more. Some months into Dad's final journey, we took a walk together in an adjacent park and although we continued to avoid any direct reference to his illness, there were silences with mountains of meaning. It has tormented me ever since that this was an opportunity to forge an honest connection but I failed to grasp the nettle, again more from concern for my mother's feelings rather than my own sensibilities.

Lin and I visited Uncle Dave and Aunt Else to bring them up to date with the situation in Romford and my father's condition. Dave was a softly spoken and thoughtful man who, like my father, would have had the intelligence to succeed in higher education and a profession without his deprived childhood and the intervention of the war. Even so, he trained as a draughtsman and engineer and had a responsible job at Ford preparing written technical data for all the models manufactured by the company. He listened intently and, although he said little, he was clearly shocked and distressed by the sad news of his older brother. Before we left, we passed small talk to lighten the conversation and he mentioned that he was still playing badminton but had pulled a muscle in his side that week.

A month or two later, I was asked to phone my mother urgently. Expecting the worst, I rang her in Romford with trepidation. My father was at the hospital, but she had some terrible news. Uncle Dave had cancer. My brain whirled with shock, but also revelation. Three brothers, the first, Richard, having died from mesothelioma; the second, George, with clinical features of mesothelioma; and the third, Dave, presenting at the same time with advanced cancer. And all three having worked with my grandfather for the asbestos company Turner & Newall, lagging pipes and boilers in power stations along the Thames. The thirty-year-plus incubation period between asbestos exposure and cancer was spot on.

My memory returned to the time that I had noticed my father picking at warts in his palm.

"Had them since I worked with the old man," he said, and dismissed my concerns.

Asbestos warts, of course – the fibres lodged in the skin, causing chronic inflammation.

And what of their sister, Eva? A gynaecological malignancy causing her death in her thirties. Weren't there stories of her joyfully running to meet her father as a toddler, sitting on his lap in the white dust covering his overalls when he returned from work? No pathologist would have considered mesothelioma in this young woman in those days. The jigsaw was almost complete when biopsies confirmed that Dave did indeed have mesothelioma. My uncle's terminal illness compounded the problems of maintaining the fragile charade as my father accused him of being uncaring in his absence and failing to make contact. Somehow, my mother and sister continued to shield him from the truth for his remaining months.

In our hall at home we have a large, heavy stone with a conical top and a six-inch-square base. It is shaped like a hobbit house and painted accordingly, with brick-red roof and green windows. It acts as a doorstop and visitors must wonder why this awkward object has such a proud position of prominence. In our study, we have a painting of the ancient boat-shaped prison in Annecy surrounded by its green moat, flowers in troughs and pretty shopfronts on walkways. The colours are lurid and the perspective slightly awry. These precious items have travelled with us around the country and are unlikely to be discarded. They were painted and given to me by patients who were terminally ill; partly in gratitude but also, I suspect, as small, enduring reminders of their lives. During the later stages of my father's illness, when he had been discharged from work and diminishing time lay heavily on his hands, my mother had a moment of inspiration and purchased some marquetry kits. Engrossed, and working hours at a time, he set to the task of constructing intricate pictures in different-coloured wood veneers – galleons in full sail, windmills on hilltops, castles in clouds. We were not a demonstrative family and he may have underestimated how much he was loved and respected. In his own way, he was leaving each of us a small memento of his time here to remember him by.

There may have been tears in private, but George projected a positive front to his loved ones and this strong, proud man was unlikely to show us his true feelings.

"Don't forget your tablets, George," said my mother with tender concern, but there was little chance of that. He had been prescribed potassium supplements to replace the large amounts lost in the litres of fluid periodically drawn from his abdomen. As his only therapeutic crutch, he took the pills religiously and it was heartbreaking to see the unrealistic faith he bestowed upon them as a life-sustaining medicine. Hope was hanging by the thinnest of threads.

We visited Dave and Else one last time a week before he died. Else spoke quietly about how she was coping and we then went to Dave's room where, in her typical no-nonsense fashion, she busied herself gently washing his face and changing his pyjama top. He was severely wasted and clearly in extremis; we were both aware that there was little time remaining. Lin and I provided only a sympathetic ear, but I believe that visit cemented our close bond with Else which has remained to this day.

At the weekend, we visited Romford. My father was still standing tall like a Marine, but he was very weak and breathless. I lay on the bed with him in the evening with my mother listening close by, and we exchanged a few words in the developing darkness. I surreptitiously felt his pulse and it was weak, thready and irregular. As he drifted in and out of sleep, I heard him whisper words which I have found difficult to forget:

"I can't dream any more."

My interpretation was that he had no more fight, his spirit was broken and he had reached the end. In the morning, he had energy enough to sit by the window and weakly wave goodbye as we departed. It was the last time we saw him alive. George died within hours of Dave on Thursday 3rd May 1979. History would record that it was a black day from every perspective.

Lin and I returned to Romford and I went to the hospital with my mother on the Friday. I took responsibility for identifying my father's body and, with my experience in the geriatric ward and dissecting room, I was not apprehensive about the proximity to death. I was uncertain of my emotional response to seeing my father, however. As it happens, I had no need to worry; he was still my dad and his face was in pale, peaceful repose. I held his hand for a moment, said quietly, "Thanks, Dad", and confirmed identification to the attendant.

We made our way to the clerk's office to collect his belongings and discuss the next step. She was sweet, kind and sensitive as she must have been many times before with grieving relatives. But then she added, "We have issued the death certificate for you to take away."

I glanced at the sheet, which stated, *1. Myocardial infarction. 2a. Carcinomatosis.*

2b. Carcinoma of bronchus.

"No, that's not correct," I said firmly, and explained the background of two brothers dying from mesothelioma. I was aware that, if there was any possibility of industrial disease, the death must be reported to the coroner and a coroner's post-mortem was legally mandated. Tissue samples would be taken and a pathologist would carefully deliberate on the microscopic material and reach a definitive diagnosis. The body would only then be released for cremation if the coroner was satisfied with the cause of death. The clerk acquiesced, and we left to continue our quiet grieving and to await the outcome.

This arrived during the following week and, to our dismay, the cause of death remained unchanged. The post-mortem material was referred to the Pneumoconiosis Medical Panel which concluded: *There is no evidence of asbestosis and the majority view is that the tumour is a carcinoma. On the evidence available there is nothing to suggest that this is a death due to industrial disease.* We were convinced that the diagnosis was wrong but I don't remember any overwhelming sense of anger or injustice in the immediate aftermath. There was no second court and we were too exhausted by the events of the previous year to take up the cudgels. Resigned to the outcome, the funeral arrangements were begun.

The ceremonies were held just a few days apart and both are very sketchy in my mind. They were fine spring days and I remember the pink blossom on the flowering cherry trees. For George's cavalcade, Fred was given the honour of accompanying the immediate family in the first limousine behind the hearse and Lin and Dorothy were in the second. We passed the General Post Office depot and briefly paused in front of the waiting postmen, who were present in such numbers that none could have remained in the building. Elderly strangers stopped in the street and doffed their hats as a mark of respect as we continued on our way. Most of the service I can barely remember apart from the hymn *Abide with Me*, which was commonly chosen to be sung at the funerals of old navy men and reminded us of Dad's footballing days. In every way, though, the whole family was physically and emotionally spent and all the tears had been cried.

9

Houseman's Tales

We returned to Nottingham and, although grief would hang heavy, I had little time to dwell. We were on our last attachments in medicine and surgery before final examinations and the pace was quickening. It was customary for senior students to perform short periods of locum work to gain experience while covering a junior house officer colleague's absence. The novices were always closely supported by more senior staff and, with no authority to prescribe, their responsibilities were limited to checking patients on the ward, seeing routine new admissions and perhaps taking blood samples. It was a rite of passage and one of a series of steps which had to be nervously traversed in the quest to become a qualified doctor.

I covered a surgical ward for the weekend. The Saturday passed without drama and when the consultant phoned me in the evening I was able to reassure him that there were no major problems. Sundays were generally quieter, and I thought that I might work my way through the medical notes to learn about the patients' backgrounds in more detail. As I settled with a cup of coffee in Sister's office, she came to me and reported that Mr Barwell was unwell. It soon became clear that this was an understatement and he was semi-conscious and hyperventilating. Simple tests rapidly revealed that he had diabetic pre-coma and, knowing my limitations, I bleeped the medical registrar on call. He appeared briskly, took control of the situation and formulated a plan for me to enact. That would fill my time for the afternoon – intensive monitoring was required, with frequent blood samples and clinical assessment. As I set to the task, the sister called me to another patient who was complaining of sharp chest pain and difficulty breathing. He was three days post-op and a blood clot on the lung was likely. I called the medical team again and a plan was formulated for me to enact. I juggled the two sick patients and kept an eye on the routine cases in the ward as well as clerking in a new admission. Several relatives were waiting to be seen and were becoming restless. Then there was a crash. Mr Turner had reached for his locker, fallen out of bed and, as it turned out, fractured his hip. I called the orthopaedic registrar.

"Welcome to my world," the houseman said, when I recounted my weekend. This is how senior students were made abruptly aware of the nature of this multitasking, high-intensity, stamina-sapping emotional roller coaster of a job which would be theirs in just a few months' time.

Final examinations came and went and, as expected, nobody failed after five years of study. We had qualified as doctors and my younger colleagues were getting used to the cachet of the title. I had technically been a doctor since being awarded a PhD, but I had rarely used the title; partly to avoid confusion with the clinical qualification and also to avoid singling myself out as having any special status over my classmates. Mind you, once we had begun our preregistration house officer year, we would be either working or sleeping, and there would be little social life outside the hospital to test our new-found professional status. We were each required to complete six months of junior posts in medicine and surgery. In those days, before working time directives, we could be in the hospital either working, on call or asleep for up to 120 hours per week. I would sometimes say goodbye to my wife on Thursday morning and greet her again on the Tuesday evening. After a delicious unbroken night's sleep, I was ready to say goodbye again the following morning. Perhaps surprisingly, however, there was a general sense of privilege amongst my colleagues, and gratitude that we were in a position to fulfil our ambitions. Of course, it was traditional for the older generation to dismiss any complaints about workload by their younger colleagues. Though its veracity cannot be confirmed, my consultant mentor, John Fletcher, told me that he worked every day but Christmas Day in the '50s – and his consultant asked him on 26th December where he had been the previous day!

I will not fall into this trap of Dickensian storytelling. Young doctors today do work shorter shifts, but the demands are even more intensive and the technical skills required a great deal higher as medical knowledge has advanced. And that is not to mention the overwhelming tsunami of form-filling and paperwork that engulfs the present-day doctor.

The downside of the long hours in terms of patient safety was self-evident. I was once close to forty-eight hours without sleep and a zombie would have appeared the life and soul of the party alongside me. The upside was that you saw every case that came into the hospital and, once seen, a condition was never forgotten. I remember clerking a patient with lymphangiosarcoma of Stewart and Treves at the Marsden; an elderly lady with a swollen arm after breast surgery. I never saw another case in the whole of my career, but I would vouch that I would still recognise it if I saw a similar patient today.

In some ways, my first house job on the genito-urinary (GU) surgical unit was a gentle introduction. GU surgeons sometimes performed very technical operations, for example, refashioning artificial bladders from a patient's small or large bowel and reconnecting all the tubes and pipes to produce an efficient path for the urine to flow. I'm sure that more elaborate procedures have now been developed but I have been out of the field for some time. The 'bread and butter' patient on the unit, however, was typically an elderly man with an enlarged prostate who required the telescopic removal of the inner part of the gland to improve urine flow. The telescope with cutting tool was inserted through the penis under general anaesthetic and the prostate chipped away from the inside. As I reach the age where such an operation sometimes becomes necessary, I'm not sure that it is a good thing to be as well informed as I am!

My duties simply entailed clerking the patients and ensuring that they were fit for the operation. The problem with older men, and women for that matter, is that they rarely have a single health problem. The surgeons were concerned with planning their operation but tended to have little knowledge of or interest in any other conditions the patient might suffer from – as long as they were fit for them to practise their surgical skills. Consequently, there was an immediate need for the new houseman to become adept at managing a host of ancillary medical problems – heart failure, raised blood pressure, diabetes mellitus, emphysema, whatever – or at least to recognise when an anaesthetist or medical registrar needed to be forewarned or called for assistance.

The consultant was a bluff Yorkshireman who was newly appointed. It is only in retrospect that one realises that new consultants will have their own insecurities and nervousness as they learn that the buck truly stops with them. Nevertheless, he was kind and gave his time freely. He took me through the one and only hands-on operation I was ever going to personally perform. Half the readership should look away now: it was an orchidectomy, surgical removal of the testes which is recommended in some patients with prostate cancer. On another occasion, I helped him undertake a more difficult operation to remove a kidney tumour. These cancers have a tendency to invade and adhere to blood vessels and, halfway through the operation, the consultant's demeanour changed rapidly.

"Artery forceps!" he barked, with just a hint of panic.

As the words came out, I watched in dismay as the cavity he was exploring filled with blood before my eyes. In a flash, the ice-queen surgical sister who was assisting had the instrument in his hand and he probed and felt blindly in the bottom of the rapidly filling reservoir. The bleeding subsided and peace and order were restored, but it was a sobering experience and served as a reminder of why sometimes our surgical colleagues seem a breed apart.

And so my houseman's year proceeded. For the next three months of my surgical attachment I worked on the breast unit, which required a special mix of empathy and sensitivity in dealing with some very anxious women, both young and old. Professor Roger Blamey became a doyen in his field and I learnt a lot. I was always likely to have more leanings towards medical specialties, however, and was looking forward to my six-month spell on the professorial unit with Mike Langman at its head.

The pattern of work on a medical firm in the early '80s was that the team had a special interest, in this case, gastroenterology, but on one day in six all acute emergency admissions were absorbed into the mix. This could include patients with coronary heart disease, pneumonia, bronchitis or endocrine disorders, for example; thyroid disease, and stroke. Complex or rarer patients with kidney disease, leukaemia or similar would be transferred to other firms but, in general, there was much less specialisation than today. Indeed, it was only a few years before that the true general physician existed; a colleague who would basically take any patient with any problem under his wing.

Given the professor's interest, I saw many patients with inflammatory bowel diseases like Crohn's disease and ulcerative colitis, which were difficult to manage in those days and are still not easy to treat today. One dramatic advance which altered clinical practice in gastroenterology virtually overnight was the discovery of the cause of peptic ulcer disease in 1982. Hitherto, stomach and duodenal ulcers were thought primarily to be due to excessive acid secretion, perhaps with a psychosomatic component. Treatment was with diet or, if severe, surgery, which could include cutting the vagus nerve which controlled acid production or resecting portions of the stomach. The discovery of the critical role of the bacterium *Helicobacter pylori* as a cause of the disease is worthy of a book chapter on its own and would earn Professor Barry Marshall a Nobel Prize. The organism had been recognised in the lining of the stomach for a generation. However, it took a special personality to swim against the tide of popular opinion and prove that the bacterium had a primary role in ulcer formation rather than as an innocent bystander in the process. Elimination of the organism with combinations of antibiotics, inhibitors of acid production and sometimes bismuth commonly resulted in cure and the role of surgery virtually disappeared overnight.

Our emergency admission days in Nottingham were frequently very busy and literally, one could not predict what patient or clinical problem would appear, day or night. Some remain in my memory to this day. A young mother with a particularly virulent strain of pneumococcal pneumonia who died despite our best efforts. The whole team was deeply affected by this loss. The young jobless man living alone who was found mysteriously comatose with a bucket of water by his bed. The level of sodium in his blood was very low and the cause became obvious – psychogenic polydipsia or water intoxication. This dangerous condition can lead to brain swelling and death and required very careful management of his fluid volume and plasma electrolytes. He passed five litres of urine shortly after admission and survived. A windsurfer who appeared with acute kidney failure and liver damage and had Weil's disease or leptospirosis; a bacterial infection caught from rat urine in still water. Again, rapid supportive care and antibiotics resulted in recovery.

Two junior housemen were appointed to each firm, one looking after those in the male ward and the other looking after female patients. My counterpart was my good friend and prospective surgeon, Graham. As I have previously described, he had already acquired a certain confidence in his own ability in keeping with his future role. On the first emergency 'take' day he received a call from a GP who said he had been to see a young man who had suffered sickness and was faint on getting out of bed. Now you would be thinking about an episode of gastroenteritis, and so would I. But not Graham.

"Hmm, sounds like Addison's disease to me," he pronounced, honing down on the potentially fatal syndrome of adrenal failure and collapsed steroid secretion which can lead to a collapsed patient. Well, this patient's symptoms would indeed do for Addison's disease, but with an annual incidence of five cases per million of the population, this would not be top of most people's list. A GP would be unlikely to diagnose a new case in his working lifetime. Need I go on? Graham's diagnostic coup meant that I was already one point behind in our competition to impress the professor, and it was only our fourth day on the firm!

My interest in medicine rather than surgery was reinforced by these varied experiences and I chose to continue training on a medical senior house officer (SHO) rotation in Nottingham. This would provide a career path and some degree of stability in our domestic life for the following two years. More specialist training would be forthcoming in cardiology, respiratory diseases, renal disorders including kidney transplantation, and endocrine disorders like diabetes mellitus.

I sat musing recently as I looked up the garden towards our cat's resting place. Over the forty years of my career in medicine, what have been the other most notable advances in addition to recognition of the role of *Helicobacter pylori* in peptic ulcer disease? Well, from a personal point of view, artificial joint replacements must come high on the list; my new ceramic-and-titanium hip having allowed me to enjoy my weekly swim without pain and with renewed vigour. The procedure has become the routine entry requirement for baby boomers about to begin their geriatric gap years. It was pioneered in the UK by Sir John Charnley in the early '60s and became one of the commonest operations performed worldwide. Would it be cardiology, where advances in surgical skill and cardiac bypass technology have enabled coronary artery grafts to become routine, interventional radiologists have become adept at inserting stents, pharmacologists have discovered statins, and public health drives have reduced the prevalence of smoking? Or perhaps haematology, where there has been greatest overlap between medicine and advancing basic science to forge new treatments for leukaemia and other serious bone marrow disorders? Antiviral therapy for HIV infection, the genetics revolution, organ transplantation?

From a practical point of view, I could make a case for developments in diagnostic imaging and radiology. In our houseman years, X-rays were developed and viewed on sheets of cellulose acetate and kept in thin cardboard envelopes which rapidly became damaged. X-ray meetings soon devolved into farce as the films, slippery as eels garnished in olive oil, slid through the fingers and fell on the floor. The remaining contents of the envelope would join their brethren as one bent down to retrieve the wayward film, and everyone would spring to their feet to help the unfortunate trying unsuccessfully to corral the sheets back into the dilapidated folder. The films often ended up upside down or the wrong way round on the viewing box – situs inversus is a very rare condition where all the internal organs are displaced in mirror image, but was surprisingly common when students were asked to put up and interpret chest X-rays.

In the modern day, all the images are digitised and freely available to anyone authorised on any desktop computer in the hospital. Radiologists are able to focus on uncertain areas, alter the orientation and highlight subtle changes. As we studied in Nottingham, we were not aware that a lecturer was steadily at work in the physics department, developing technology which would transform diagnostic imaging. Sir Peter Mansfield was another eleven-plus failure and late developer who achieved far greater accolades than I could ever aspire to. In 2003 he was awarded the Nobel Prize for Physiology or Medicine for his work on magnetic resonance imaging (MRI). It is now well known that this technique uses powerful magnetic fields and radio waves to produce images of unrivalled detail to visualise tissues and organs in the body. It has particular application in viewing the brain, nervous system and musculoskeletal structures including the spine. An added advantage is that it does not involve exposing the patient to radiation. Professor Mansfield was involved in all aspects of the development but made a particular contribution to the mathematical analysis of the radio waves which allowed the images to be generated.

During my time, the successful application of computerisation to medical imaging was an exception rather than the rule when it came to the introduction of information technology (IT) into the health service. I remember in 2002 the consultant body being called to attend a meeting on a major new initiative to computerise patient records, store all NHS data and promote 'paperless' care pathways including electronic prescribing and appointment-booking services. A director had been appointed from the private sector on an enormous salary and the presenter from the IT department was brimming with enthusiasm and could barely contain his excitement. The consultants, meanwhile, were looking at each other knowingly and with more than a trace of scepticism. Real-time digitisation of the chaotic activity that characterised the day-to-day functions of a busy hospital? Who was going to enter all the data? Would they know all the complex terminology? How would they do the coding? Could urgent information be accessed immediately? And how could all the ad hoc systems already in place be replaced or melded into the new all-encompassing network? Technical challenges, contractual problems and legal disputes added to the confusion and delay. The whole project was considered to be a fiasco at a cost of £10 billion, and the NHS director of the initiative left and quietly found his way back to a lucrative private sector job.

The loud chirrup of the cardiac arrest bleep woke me abruptly from my slumbers. Like the urgent cry of a baby at night, it was designed to make it impossible to ignore. The bleep gave the location of the incident and I leapt out of the warm bed, threw on some clothes, grabbed my white coat and ran.

By the time I arrived, my registrar, David, was already at the foot of the bed, standing with calm authority and directing the well-rehearsed drama unfolding. We were in the coronary care unit; the place to be if you have a cardiac arrest as the efficient and professional nursing staff were well drilled in the routine of immediate resuscitation. Shocks were given, heart rhythms checked, cardiac output monitored and stabilising drugs injected before Dave pronounced that the patient was no longer in danger and we could return to bed. In the morning, we would wake wondering whether the single-act play we had witnessed had actually happened.

On the ward round at 8.30am sharp, Professor Langman was delighted with our efforts; all the more so because the patient was the juniors coach at Notts County Cricket Club and tutored the prof's son. The coach made an excellent recovery and, a few months later, we all received a generous invitation to visit Trent Bridge, be treated to lunch and watch a first-class county match. I can still remember Derek Randall, the English Test match player, hopping and fidgeting in the covers, as was his manner. It was always satisfying to be part of a successful resuscitation team, but this one had an unexpected delayed gratification.

Perhaps surprisingly, one of my favourite times to be working long shifts in the hospital were the quiet hours between midnight and 2am. Empty corridors apart from an occasional night cleaner, greeted with a nod, or a trolley in the distance carrying an emergency patient to theatre. Otherwise, the hospital's main arteries were devoid of life as I plied between darkened wards to have a final check on my patients or respond to a persistent bleep. Nurses, porters and junior doctors entered a supportive fellowship at night where relationships loosened in the absence of the high-intensity pressures of a daytime workload. Time to have a whispering coffee with a night sister in a dimly lit office, or pass a few words with the radiology technician as you followed a patient to an empty X-ray department to rapidly review a film. The hospital did not have an A&E department, which often resemble bedlam between these hours. And it was a culture shock to enter the intensive care unit, where day and night have no meaning.

On emergency take days around this time, when the bulk of urgent patients had been assessed and stabilised, and treatment plans put in place, four or five of us would retire for brief respite to the canteen, still open for a hot cooked meal. Or a game of *Space Invaders* in the junior doctors' mess before bed and, almost inevitably, disturbed sleep. Both these gestures of generosity towards a committed young workforce are long gone, like hospital consultants' dining rooms, easy victims of cuts made using the excuse of eliminating costs not directly benefiting patients. But how can providing a young doctor with a decent meal after an eighteen-hour shift not benefit patients, or allowing busy consultants a confidential refuge to meet and discuss difficult cases not be cost-effective? In later years I would balk at discussing problem patients in hospital corridors, but it was one of the few informal places I could meet senior colleagues in the atomised structure of a major teaching hospital.

I had made a mistake. Not one to cause death or major injury, but definitely a mistake. In a state of ignorance and overconfidence, I had used the notoriously unreliable fluid balance charts rather than accurate daily weight measurements to calculate the fluid replacement in a sick patient with kidney disease. Senior house officers (SHOs) always need keeping an eye on as they commonly have a little too much knowledge allied precariously with rather too little clinical experience. The electrolytes, fluid volume and acid-base numbers in the patient's body had become unbalanced and threatened to lead to heart failure or worse. It was corrected without drama, but it was a close shave. I have seen much finer doctors than me make rare out-of-character errors which were career-threatening.

Mike, the medical registrar, was kind and sympathetic but, with diplomacy, did not understate the potentially serious nature of the action. He quelled the emotion of the situation and gently defused my mixture of embarrassment, defensiveness and regret. Nevertheless, he ensured I learnt the lesson. In retrospect, of course, working on a punishing 120-hours-per-week rota was bound to involve walking a tightrope some of the time. I'm surprised that, even under this brutal workload, the number of significant errors was very small. I was always grateful to Mike for his sympathetic approach to a young houseman slightly out of his depth. His capacity for dealing with problems with a safe pair of hands and diplomacy would no doubt help him in the future when, as a cancer specialist, he became a senior figure and government spokesman at the Department of Health.

It was a Wednesday afternoon a few months later and everything was right with the world. I was driving in sunshine through green tranquillity along the Nottingham Road, heading for Newstead Abbey Park where a small cottage hospital sat at the edge of my spiritual home. Once a week as an SHO I would leave the chaotic frenzy of the teaching hospital and spend a peaceful few hours without the bleep at the convalescence unit. If you were recovering from a serious illness, looking across a rippling wheat field towards the trees bordering the serenity of the park was a good place to be. My duties were light; checking the odd patient causing concern, rewriting a few drug charts or completing a brief discharge summary. There was time to have tea and a natter with a nurse grateful to see a medic who could deal with any minor issues.

The hospital, a former sanatorium, served a critical purpose within the community despite its low-key appearance. Patients too poorly to be at home but too well to be in a high-dependency setting could take a few extra days to recover. Older patients waiting for social services to reconnect at home could be cared for in a quiet and supportive ambience. Others might have relatives who were grateful for a short interlude to adjust their lives to a homecoming loved one. Cancer patients could be given care in a gentler environment to provide their family with a brief period of respite. For others, a short window of inpatient nursing could be used to monitor and stabilise their condition after abrupt adjustments to medication for heart failure, diabetes or asthma. Thoughtless acts like discharging an elderly patient with little family support, to an empty house devoid of food or warmth just before a long bank holiday, could be avoided. The key benefit of the cottage hospital was that it acted as a pressure valve to allow the major hospital to function at optimal efficiency. And the slower pace meant that staff could have those extra moments to deal with small but nevertheless important concerns of the patient; precious moments so difficult to measure on a spreadsheet. Most importantly, they reduced the chance of patients bouncing back into expensive teaching hospital beds with unresolved or relapsing problems.

By the beginning of the next decade, these care needs were met so effectively elsewhere in Nottingham that Newstead Hospital was demolished in 1992. Strange, then, that, in 2014, the head of NHS England, Simon Stephens, signalled support for the re-establishment of cottage hospitals, and during a debate on the issue, Earl Howe, then Parliamentary Undersecretary for Health, was reported in *Hansard* as saying, *they [cottage hospitals] allow large hospitals to safely discharge patients into more appropriate care, freeing up beds in major hospitals for people who need them.*

While I was driving to see my patients at Newstead, someone in a local strategy meeting, with a forceful personality, long on ambition and short on vision, must have uttered those fateful words, "The status quo is not an option."

Evidence-based medicine has come a long way over the years; evidence-based management, not so much.

Although I described earlier rare gifts with poignant messages from patients approaching death, it must be said that most presents were given in thanks and gratitude for more successful outcomes. I still have a bottle of sherry from 1982 which carries a note: *Thank you for a miracle*. It was given to me as a houseman by the wife of an elderly man with legionnaires' disease, and it was indeed an unlikely recovery after several weeks spent on a ventilator. As the most junior member of the team, she saw me every day even though all the significant life-saving decisions were made by my more senior colleagues on the firm. Not to mention the important roles of the medical and nursing teams in the intensive care unit, and that of the paramedical staff contributing to the man's recovery. I was the human face of the joint effort, however, and I took the bottle with good grace on their behalf. I very much doubt it is palatable now, but I have no regrets about swapping a moment's pleasure of alcohol for a lifelong memento.

Following rare abuses, gifts from patients are now strictly limited and must be rigorously declared with an appropriate tick box. In those early days, however, common sense and reliance on trust and professionalism prevailed. One morning, early in my career as a consultant, my telephone rang and the female voice at the other end of the line identified herself as a consultant rheumatologist – calling from Australia. Her daughter would be passing by my hospital on her way to join her husband on a small, remote island where he worked as a custodian of a bird sanctuary. Would I be able to see her for some medical advice? Now, this was beginning to sound increasingly far-fetched. As reflected by numerous comedies on television, devilry is never far away in medical settings. I remembered as a very green houseman being on call for emergency medical patients when I received a message from a mischievous colleague warning me to prepare for a holiday coach party of haemophiliac patients who had been involved in a crash on the M1. Nevertheless, despite my reservations, I affirmed my willingness to provide a favour for my Australian colleague.

In fact, everything turned out to be true; the young woman was seen, her minor problem addressed, and I thought nothing more about the episode. A few weeks later, a wooden box arrived containing two bottles of wine from my grateful colleague. Delighted, I took the gift home and Lin and I determined to drink one of the bottles with a couple we had invited over for a takeaway Chinese meal that weekend. None of us were wine buffs but we all agreed that the wine was enjoyable, if a little on the heavy side. It would be perhaps six months later when, as we idly watched a television programme on the world's greatest wines, a bottle of Penfolds Grange came into view. *It can't be – it is!* At £200 per bottle, we had drunk it with a Chinese takeaway. I guess the Fortnum & Mason label on the box should have given it away.

Jade was an intelligent young woman in her early thirties who had developed severe aplastic anaemia. In this rare condition, the body's immune system destroys the stem cells in the bone marrow, which becomes empty and devoid of function. The production of red cells for carrying oxygen, white cells for defence against infection, and platelets which promote blood clotting is switched off and, without treatment, patients can rapidly die from infection or bleeding. A number of therapies are possible, but bone marrow transplantation is the preferred option, particularly if the patient is young and a tissue-matched brother or sister is available. Jade was fortunate: her younger brother was a match and she would go on to be cured of her condition.

She was sitting with her husband one day, receiving a blood transfusion and munching on a banana prior to the transplant. In complete innocence, I complimented her on eating a healthy diet and mentioned that I was also very keen on fruit. We compared notes on our favourite tipples. Some months later, in the week before Christmas, we had an unexpected knock on the front door. I was confronted by a man struggling to hold the most enormous box of fruit imaginable.

"This is from my boss, Mr Smith," explained the man as my daughters appeared, wide-eyed, at my side. "He said that you can expect one every year while you are in the city." And he proved true to his word. I promise that I had no idea when I complimented his wife that her husband owned a large fruit wholesale business!

You may notice that there is little mention of my wife or two new daughters over this period. This is not due to bashfulness on their part. We knew that maintaining a normal family life would be very difficult during the three years I spent doing house jobs. It required a wife with very special qualities to sustain it and for us to come out at the other end of the experience with a stronger bond. If I was at home, awake and present in body, I was barely present in mind. Photographs of that time invariably show a pallid fellow with a bleep in his top pocket, having just come in from work or just about to leave. In fact, my second daughter's first words were not "Dad" or "Daddy", but, "Him coming, him coming", as the vaguely remembered stranger crawled up the path.

In addition to medical duties, I was preparing for postgraduate professional examinations. Membership of the Royal College of Physicians (MRCP) was a stepping stone to traverse before a career could be progressed in any medical specialty involving direct care of patients. The MRCP was composed of two parts. Part I was a written paper, which I passed at the second attempt. Part II was a clinical exam which tested practical clinical skills in more depth, including history-taking, examining the patient, and discussing diagnosis and management. There were also short spot cases, for example, a patient with a rash, a heart murmur, a neurological sign or a rheumatoid hand. The so-called long case was where the capricious gods who control destiny in clinical exams could exert the vagaries of their mood.

At my first attempt, the case was an elderly lady with something of an old chestnut for candidates: mixed mitral valve disease with what should have been a classic history of symptoms and typical heart murmurs. Unfortunately, she rambled and went off at tangents to such a degree that I thought she had been preprogrammed by the examiners to obfuscate at any opportunity. Worse was to come.

It was November and a cold day. Why would this be relevant? Well, Russian dolls would give a hint, or perhaps pass the parcel! Layer upon layer of winceyette and a corset like armour. Two hours, rather than forty minutes, wouldn't have been enough to reach the Holy Grail of her chest wall and the precious sound of her heart murmurs. At the next exam in Glasgow, on the other hand, the patient was a middle-aged chap with rheumatoid arthritis, who gave a wink as I came into his bay and seemed to be complicit in seeking to impress the examiners. He gave a perfect history and even pointed out the odd clinical feature that I had missed!

10

Celtic Adventures

"Oh, bach, you shouldn't have, that's lovely!" said the miner's wife in the musical, lyrical birdsong of the Welsh Valleys. I was in Mountain Ash, a mining village which was less beautiful than its name implied, but full of friendly, down-to-earth people who welcomed me warmly into their modest homes. They were Welsh mining stock through and through, but were in the middle of a courageous battle for survival; a struggle which they would eventually lose. I was visiting during the 1984 miners' strike and the families were fighting an assault on their culture and livelihood. I had returned to this woman's home to take further blood samples, and brought her two small tricycles no longer used by my daughters. She could find a use for them herself as we approached Christmas, or add them to the local fundraising efforts.

The story began when I was reviewing a blood film in the haematology laboratory of the University Hospital in Cardiff where I had been appointed as a clinical lecturer. I had identified two brothers with low platelet counts in their blood; tiny cells which contribute to the formation of a clot at the site of a wound. Increased bruising and bleeding can result if the numbers are reduced, particularly after surgery or injury. Checking other members of the extended family revealed a further eight males with the condition. This was obviously a genetic disorder, and one carried on the X chromosome by the mother and showing itself in the sons like haemophilia. Tracking the family members gave me the opportunity to explore the Valleys and have the privilege of getting to know their people. News of my interest spread amongst the kindred and, because of the way the Valleys fan out geographically from the capital, I found myself communicating between branches that had not seen each other for years – separated on each side of the mountains. I couldn't have hoped for a better way of immersing myself in true Welsh culture.

Many will know Cardiff as a large, cosmopolitan and multicultural city but, with the Arms Park and the River Taff as powerful symbols at its centre, its Welsh heritage is plain to see. Nevertheless, we were accepted into the warmth of its community without question, and vice versa. A new set of friends were added to our old ones and we established all the routines of a fresh life in a new city. And our young daughters would take on the personas of an Angharad and a Ffion and replace their early dialects of Alan Sillitoe with the lilt of Dylan Thomas. Our house was chosen on a number of criteria, but the most important was its short distance from the hospital. Although no longer the resident on call, I had to plan for regular trips to the haematology ward in the early hours to deal with problems that could not be handled over the phone. We lived not far from the Welsh National Museum of History at St Fagans, and the girls could learn about their new home through the authentic Welsh dwellings that have been transported to the site, complete with interiors that are accurately portrayed. And on special days in school, they dressed in traditional Welsh costume with shawl, apron, tall black hat, a single daffodil and a beaming smile.

I have previously referenced the concept of yin and yang, and this can equally be applied to the peripatetic life of a junior doctor. Moving to different locations, particularly with a young family, was always hard work. The argument from a professional point of view, however, was that it provided experience of working in different centres with alternative approaches and facilities. Senior teaching staff would have their own particular interests and, like a jackdaw, skills and knowledge could be absorbed from the different sources. In Cardiff we were also pleased to be close to the coast again, where we could take day trips to Southerndown, the Ogmore Valley, Porthcawl, or further afield to the Gower.

For those who are unfamiliar, haematology is the study of diseases that affect the production of healthy blood cells and the large variety of disorders of the bone marrow where they are made. As previously mentioned, the most important cells in the marrow are the stem cells. These primitive 'seed cells' are rare and difficult to identify, but generally never become exhausted. They provide a constant source of all the different types of blood cells produced by the marrow over the course of a person's lifetime. They are also the critical cells that become seriously defective in malignant disorders like leukaemia, and which must be replaced by those from a healthy donor in a bone marrow transplant. In addition to anaemias and leukaemias, haematologists have traditionally managed patients with blood clotting disorders like haemophilia, and have overall responsibility for the safe provision of blood for transfusion by the hospital blood bank.

In the 1980s, the specialty underwent something of a transformation. In my early years as a student, the consultant haematologists worked almost exclusively in the laboratory, which was generally situated between the hospital laundry and the boiler house. They rarely ventured onto the ward and patients with blood disorders were looked after by general physicians who had a special interest in the subject. However, a combination of factors changed the status quo. An explosion of basic science meant that the diagnosis and treatment of such patients became much more complicated and demanding – beyond the expertise of a generalist. And prospective young haematologists like myself became more interested in clinical matters and equipped ourselves with MRCP as part of our training. Specialisation was only to increase over the coming decades as treatments like bone marrow transplantation became widely applied and involved greater use of complex technology. Knowledge and skills in all these aspects of the subject would be acquired during my training in Wales. At the end of this time I would need the stamina to complete one final hurdle of exams – Membership of the Royal College of Pathologists.

"Dad, you are on the TV!" cried my seven-year-old daughter in her newly acquired lilt.

"Don't be silly," I replied – and then had a second look. She was right; behind the surgical mask, and with spectacles perched on my nose, you could just recognise my features. I hadn't realised the clip of me taking bone marrow from a donor in the operating theatre was going to be made available by the university to the BBC Local News Centre just up the road in Llandaff. Later, the footage would often be trotted out if there was a human-interest story about someone receiving a transplant or needing a donor.

Bone marrow transplantation is actually rather unsophisticated. About a litre and a half of liquid bone marrow is aspirated by large needles from the pelvis of the donor under general anaesthetic and, following processing to concentrate the white cells and reduce the volume, the product is simply infused back into a vein of the recipient like a blood transfusion. The stem cells are clever and home in on the niche in the recipient's marrow cavity, begin dividing and eventually replace the patient's blood cell production. The recipient must be in remission from his or her leukaemia, and they are pretreated with irradiation and high doses of chemotherapy. This makes space for the incoming donor stem cells and suppresses the patient's immunity to ensure that the graft is not rejected. The hard part is keeping the patient alive while the new marrow regenerates when no new blood cells are being produced and the recipient is at risk of life-threatening infections, bleeding and other serious complications.

When my consultant in Cardiff first decided that we should start performing transplants in our unit, we had virtually no experience between us. Rather than the highly regulated manufacturing processes and standards employed today, the bone marrow was manipulated in a corner of one of the research laboratories. At the end of my career, dedicated transplant units with high-tech facilities and spaceship control panels to regulate the environment were built. In the early days we had to coerce the anaesthetists to allow us to use a side room in the intensive care unit; a space which had previously been used to store old equipment. It was several months before we realised that the direction of the filter for the clean air supply to the room was the wrong way round and contaminated air was being sucked into the area.

And yet the first ten transplants were fantastically successful and all the patients flew through their ordeal. Whether this was beginners' luck or the fact that the cases were highly selected to give the best chance of avoiding complications, I'm not sure.

Bone marrow transplantation is a double-edged sword. It undoubtedly led to major improvements in the outlook of patients with serious blood disorders, and it can be commonly curative in those with, for example, leukaemia, aplastic anaemia or sickle-cell anaemia. However, in essence it is a crude procedure and the mortality rate is high. Long-term complications may be life-changing and debilitating. Sometimes it is necessary to quote patients a 20% chance of not surviving the procedure and leaving the transplant unit alive. On the other hand, if the chance of cure from a particular leukaemia is 5% without it, the decision does not appear quite so difficult. No doubt in the future, scientific advances will render transplant units obsolete and they will be thought of as we now remember sanatoriums for patients with tuberculosis.

Acute promyelocytic leukaemia (APML) is an example of how

stem cell transplantation can be superseded as a first-line treatment by new developments in drug therapy. Acute leukaemias in general develop rapidly over a matter of weeks and, if untreated, patients succumb in rather less time. The marrow can be replaced by up to 100% of malignant cells which are identical and have no function. Before treatment is commenced, APML is rather more adept at killing patients than other types because there is a severe risk of bleeding. We once diagnosed a young woman based on a GP's blood test in the morning, and the police found her dead on her settee at home in the afternoon. In 1988, a Chinese group reported a large series of patients who responded to a drug called all-trans retinoic acid, an agent not so different chemically from vitamin A and carotene, which give carrots their orange colour. This was met with initial scepticism but was later verified in the West. By combining with gentle chemotherapy, the large majority of patients are now cured of this leukaemia. It was very satisfying towards the end of my career to have so many waiting to see me in the outpatients' clinic, knowing that few would have made it there in previous years. There was further good news for the handful of patients who relapse. In the late 1990s, a 'new' agent became available to treat patients with APML, again first reported by a Chinese group. Not one developed in the molecular biology laboratories of pharmaceutical companies, however – more inspired by the cosmetics of ancient painted ladies and Renaissance poisoners. Arsenic in low doses was shown to selectively interfere with the biochemical processes driving this leukaemia, and has provided another very important weapon in the armoury.

He sat on his mother's lap, eyeing me suspiciously before his face broke into a broad grin. A cherubic eighteen-month-old infant with soft grey eyes and a blond mop of hair.

"I thought it was time I introduced you to Ben," Eleri said with a proud smile.

We had known each other for a long time, seven years or more, since I was first appointed in Cardiff. The undulating melody of her Welsh accent reminded me of the time we first met and the words she uttered then. At the age of seventeen, she presented with acute lymphoblastic leukaemia. I remembered entering her cubicle to introduce myself and being confronted by a pale, sickly-looking girl with her nervous father by her side. Gently, I explained the diagnosis and how we were going to manage her treatment – avoiding too much information at this stage because their minds would be in turmoil. After I had finished, Eleri turned to me to raise an important point about the plan.

"Does that mean I won't be able to go clubbing tonight?' she asked, before again burying her head in the pillow.

The chemotherapy was intensive, and we shared many ups and downs together. Eventually, after six months of treatment, which at times took her to the edge of survival, we were able to enter the maintenance stage – mostly tablets, which could be prescribed on an outpatient basis and continued for a further year. Two of the drugs used, methotrexate and cyclophosphamide, I had been familiar with since my PhD days. At that time, I was studying their effects on the bone marrow and the dynamics of recovery after the cells were damaged. It was critical information for the development of these agents as treatments for leukaemia.

The studies involved the use of rats and mice bred in the laboratory, and here I realise I am entering a difficult area. Many people, of course, have very strong views on the use of animals in medical research. It goes without saying that the process should be closely monitored to ensure animal welfare, and careful ethical assessment made to justify the benefits of the research undertaken. I guess it is a societal and personal decision as to whether the ends justify the means. There is certainly a strong emotional component; on visits to pharmaceutical companies I saw puppies and kittens used in pharmacology research and felt that it would have been very difficult for me to undertake such studies – even though compliance with regulations was exemplary and I knew the research was vital.

What can be said for certain is that, over many years as a doctor, I have never had a parent ask me to refrain from treating their child with meningitis because the antibiotics were tested on animals. And I have never had a husband ask me not to treat his wife with cancer because the chemotherapy drugs were tested on animals.

Sometimes the answers to difficult ethical questions are not clear-cut. At my desk in the leukaemia clinic, whenever I mused on such dilemmas, I imagined looking into Ben's twinkling grey eyes for guidance.

By its nature, haematology is not without its emergency-room drama. Treating patients with septic shock and life-threatening haemorrhage is part of the daily routine on a haematology ward, much like a GP seeing patients with back pain or managing insulin requirements in diabetics. However, there were also patients with chronic blood diseases like myeloproliferative disorders and low-grade lymphomas, which only progress and evolve over many years. Reviewing such patients in clinic commonly required a quick enquiry about their state of health, a brief examination and a glance at the blood counts measured that day. Consequently, there was ample time to get to know the patients on a personal level and, since these conditions tend to affect the elderly, there were many stories to tell.

I had a special bond with an octogenarian and former trade unionist who had personal memories of meetings with Nye Bevan and insights into his character. There were also welcome visits from a former Lord Mayor, who was full of energy and can-do spirit despite advancing years and deteriorating health. And a Knight of the Realm who, with his delightful lady wife, was suddenly thrust into an unaccustomed landscape of dependency and need. He had left it late to recognise that wealth, power and status mean nothing when a fatal illness strikes and death comes knocking. An irrepressible businessman was another who was not content to twiddle his thumbs in retirement. Unfazed as his horizon inched closer, he was determined to set up one last enterprise between pulses of chemotherapy. This 'never-say-die' attitude was typical of many elderly patients. I particularly recall a sprightly man in his nineties, entering the last stages of his leukaemia, who told me that he would not make his next clinic appointment. I surmised that he was beginning to show calm acceptance of his advancing illness, until he told me that it was because he was going on a walking holiday. On his return, I expected tales of gentle strolls along the promenade in Torquay but, instead, he was full of the wild wanderings he had enjoyed with his family in the Azores.

There are perhaps fifty or more different subtypes of leukaemia and it is the haematologist's job to recognise and treat each of them. Rhys was an architect close to the age of retirement who was diagnosed with chronic lymphocytic leukaemia; another example of a grumbling condition which slowly progresses over a number of years. Often such patients stay well, but anaemia or serious infections can intervene. At the time of first seeing him, a limited number of treatments were available but they probably did little to delay the fateful day. Rhys had married late and had a twelve-year-old daughter.

One day, he appeared troubled and, though initially reticent, eventually enquired, in a wistful voice, "Will I be here to see my daughter off to university, Dr Standen?"

I hesitated for a moment before replying, "Fifty-fifty, I guess", perhaps erring just on the side of over-optimism to maintain a positive spirit.

He seemed relieved.

As it happens, chronic lymphocytic leukaemia is an example of a disorder where, every few years, a new treatment would appear and, as resistance developed to one, a further option could be offered. Rhys not only achieved his wish, but he also saw his daughter's graduation day. Perhaps the much-maligned pharmaceutical companies should occasionally receive some well-earned credit.

"Hi, Graham!" said the tall man with a shock of red hair and a surprised expression of recognition.

I was a little surprised myself. Looking after patients for many years and sharing testing moments of drama and emotion, I was used to being on first-name terms with some of my flock. It's all a matter of context. Looking at the middle-aged chap in the side-room bed, however, I was desperately trying to place him and the reason for his familiarity.

"I'm James – you were the left back and I was the right back in our hall football team in the '70s."

Of course! And I was briefly transported back to the cold, bleak university playing fields on the banks of the Trent.

This was desperately sad. James had chronic myeloid leukaemia, which is a wolf in sheep's clothing. At that time in the early '80s, the disease was relatively benign and easily managed in the first few years after diagnosis, but in most patients the condition inevitably transformed to an untreatable and fatal acute leukaemia after five, and virtually all were dead after ten. James' leukaemia had transformed, and the outcome was predictable.

In later years, timely bone marrow transplantation would be curative for this disorder, and in the late 1990s the pharmaceutical company Novartis came up with a real gem in the form of imatinib. Not chemotherapy, but a drug with few side effects, designed from first principles and a knowledge of the genetic basis of the condition. The agent suppresses the leukaemia so effectively that barely one abnormal cell in a million can be detected in the bone marrow, and the survival of patients at ten years is now the same as healthy individuals of similar age. Sadly, these options came too late for my good friend and fellow footballer. However, imatinib could be added to the list of major advances in my medical career.

Once a year as a senior doctor, I would travel to a major foreign conference to catch up on all the new developments in haematology. Despite my wife's suspicions that these were corporate jollies, the days were long, with lectures starting at 8.30am and finishing at 6pm. Usually, however, the organisers arranged for one afternoon to be free and I would either take a city tour, wander unfamiliar streets alone, or focus on one specific landmark or place of interest. In Dallas, I saw the grassy knoll and the Texas School Book Depository, but was put off venturing outside the hotel alone after I watched from my window as a mobile intensive care unit screeched to a halt and collected a bleeding victim. In Atlanta I avoided the Coca-Cola Museum, but went to a superb aquarium which, at the time, was the largest in the world. The Hofburg Palace in Vienna, the Picasso Museum in Barcelona and, in Frankfurt, we were taken for a meal at the exclusive Schlosshotel Kronberg, formerly home to the German Empress Victoria, eldest daughter of Queen Victoria – much to the annoyance of my wife, the historian, who was at home looking after the children. I queued for two hours to enter the Uffizi Gallery in Florence, which took most of my free time.

In Paris, I met my PhD supervisor Nick Blackett, who worked there in his later years, and it would be the last time I saw him as we sat chatting on the steps of La Grande Arche de la Défense in the June sunshine. In the evening, our hosts took us to the Crazy Horse cabaret show, known for its semi-nude dancers. It wouldn't have been my first choice, but I needn't have worried. There was more eroticism conveyed by Julie Andrews in *The Sound of Music*, and the Terracotta Warriors in Xi'an showed more varied facial expressions and personality than the monotonous row of smiling mannequins on the stage. It was a warm night and, as someone unaccustomed to alcohol, the two glasses of wine were beginning to have an effect. To my embarrassment I had been placed at the edge of the floor show, but the proximity of the dancers did nothing to increase their allure. However, as the spectacle entered its final stages, I began to have a weird out-of-body experience in the darkness. For a brief moment, I had the sensation of floating and looking down on my colleagues at the table. Was this the harbinger of a further breakdown, or a religious experience to threaten my apatheism? No – the front legs of my chair overlapped the great revolving central portion of the stage, which was imperceptibly rising for the finale of the show! As I recognised the cause of my levitation, the chair came off the stage and I crashed back to the floor. The ground was rising beneath my feet, whereas I would have preferred it to have opened up for me to fall into and hide my blushes!

At another conference I sat at a wooden picnic table in a field on Lüneburg Heath in the north of Germany. It was late in the evening in mid June, and still light in this northern latitude. We were just a mile or two from where the German forces unconditionally surrendered to the Allies under Field Marshal Montgomery at the end of the Second World War. I had Professor Peter Duesberg, University of California, Berkeley, to my left and Professor Mel Greaves FRS of the Institute of Cancer Research in London to my right. On the table close by sat Bob Gallo, who would narrowly miss sharing the Nobel Prize in 2008 for discovering the HIV virus with Luc Antoine Montagnier, a French virologist, Françoise Barré-Sinoussi and Harald zur Hausen – who I think were also at the meeting. As a junior doctor, I sat quietly and listened; not for the first time wondering what a small boy from Pettits Lane School was doing in such hallowed company.

Driven by Teutonic wanderlust, the Wilsede organisers planned the meeting in a rustic and isolated village on the heath. It was at the threshold of the discovery of the HIV virus as the cause of AIDS, and the event captured this pivotal moment in science. Even at this early stage, Professor Duesberg, who was a highly respected scientist, was convinced that the HIV virus was not the causative organism in the disease. He has remained adamant in his views over the years, despite mounting evidence to the contrary. As we have seen, there is always a need to have individuals swim against the tide, but generally at some point, mounting support for a hypothesis becomes so overwhelming that a consensus is achieved. In Professor Duesberg's eyes, this point has never been reached. My only other memory of the meeting was less erudite. I had forgotten to pack a razor and, in the back of beyond, there was no opportunity to purchase one. By the time I returned home I was unrecognisable to the family and they thought I had taken the rustic theme too far.

Bryn tottered into the day unit and sat down heavily in the chair.

"Long walk from the car park," he said as he caught his breath. Thin, pale and sweating; a nineteen-year-old in a ninety-year-old body. The silhouette of a muscular frame was still present, but severe back pain had finally prevented him from continuing his work at the pithead. A routine blood count showed anaemia and prompted the phone call to his mother, but that didn't tell the half of it. He had been sick for months, but stoicism and the macho environment of the mine meant that he had avoided seeking help. A quick examination pointed the way, with clusters of enlarged lymph nodes under the arms and in the groin, and the normally shy spleen hidden behind the ribs could be felt easily in the upper abdomen. A CT scan confirmed that nodes were enlarged throughout his body, with some eroding his spine, and a week later a biopsy report showed Hodgkin's disease, as we suspected.

The treatment of Hodgkin's lymphoma has been yet another triumph of twentieth-century medicine, and the large majority of cases with less extensive disease are cured by chemotherapy and radiotherapy. In the early 1940s two young pharmacologists from Yale called Goodman and Gilman (the very same!) found that nitrogen mustard, a less volatile precursor of mustard gas, shrunk the tumours of lymphoma patients, and so the clinical science of chemotherapy was born. With other significant discoveries made at the Royal Marsden Hospital and major cancer research institutes in the States, combinations of anti-cancer drugs first found a role in the treatment and cure of hitherto fatal tumours. However, advanced Stage IV Hodgkin's disease remains a challenge, with perhaps only two thirds of patients currently surviving. After Bryn had received eight rounds of intensive chemotherapy it was time to wait and watch; secretly willing him to reach the five-year plateau of the survival curve, after which patients rarely relapsed. Those memories of our first encounter remained fresh in my mind as I welcomed the strapping twenty-six-year-old into my clinic room for a last visit before my time in Cardiff was at an end.

Professor Arthur Bloom was one of the most renowned of the clinicians and scientists working in Cardiff, and was known throughout the world for his work and commitment to the field of haemophilia. He was a short and balding man who would not have stood out in a crowd. But he was a great teacher who was held in high regard by his patients and deeply respected by all the colleagues who worked with him. It was a special pleasure to accompany him at international meetings and bask in his reflected aura as young researchers and clinicians from around the globe sought him out to discuss difficult cases or his views on the latest trends in the field. When Arthur and his wife had a summer gathering at their house, everyone was invited from consultant colleagues to the lowliest young technician. He was a father figure to the young haemophiliac patients from the Welsh Valleys, whom he had known and cared for since they were infants.

Arthur had seen the whole history of the management of this condition, and described how, in the 1950s, only fresh blood and plasma were available for treatment. This had little benefit and patients suffered frequent bleeds into joints and muscles, which could keep them bed-bound for several months. Or they would succumb to internal bleeding, most commonly in the brain. Children with haemophilia would grow up with limited schooling, poor career prospects and disabled by chronic joint damage. After the missing coagulation factor was identified as factor VIII, more concentrated products became available through the '70s and '80s and the purity and efficacy of the material improved. The quality of life of haemophiliac patients was transformed beyond all measure but, of course, very dark clouds were forming on the horizon. A large proportion of the factor VIII was purchased from America, where blood donors of questionable background were paid to source the plasma. Large batches were pooled, and HIV and hepatitis viruses were being transmitted. The outcome is known by all, and the consequences still resonate.

It would not be the only example in this era where government action was needed to scrutinise and interrogate potential conflicts between the commercial interests of multinational companies and public health. In hindsight, self-sufficiency for the product should have been an absolute priority. Nevertheless, clear explanations for the cause of this catastrophe are still being sought and the results of a statutory public enquiry are currently awaited. The clinical science at the time was a jumbled mass of kaleidoscope crystals, and much work was needed before clear patterns would emerge. During the 1980s, knowledge about HIV was still accumulating and a specific test for detecting hepatitis C was only developed in 1989. Even when contamination was beyond doubt, the level of threat was not immediately understood, and though the limited quantity of UK-derived factor VIII was safer, it was still not devoid of risk. Haemophiliac patients and their doctors were between a rock and a hard place: an intolerable dilemma of administering either cruder and less effective products containing uncertain quantities of factor VIII, with a possible outcome of chronic pain, disability or even death from bleeding; or prescribing potent imported factor VIII concentrate that posed potentially serious and, as it turned out, fatal health risks. This was a national tragedy for the large number of haemophiliac patients who lost their lives, a devastating outcome for their families and a sad end to the careers of many senior doctors and haemophilia centre directors who had dedicated their lives to their care. Arthur Bloom died suddenly in 1992 at the age of sixty-two years. It is of little solace to the families damaged by this bleak episode that safe, pure factor VIII is now synthesised by genetic engineering, and that the day when haemophilia will be cured by gene therapy is not far off.

The currency of success for an academic doctor at a university hospital is the number of major papers in influential medical journals that can be published over the course of each year. I was fortunate in having my name attached to a reasonable number of significant articles on haematology during my career. For doctors in training, however, short reports of interesting patients with a broadly educational intent were encouraged as a way of introducing writing skills and the orderly assembly of knowledge. These brief articles have little status or credibility in academic circles, but could nevertheless prove valuable. Two such reports come to mind that I was quite proud of.

The first was an elderly lady who presented with an enormous bruise on her upper arm. Not so unusual, but a few days later she developed a similar bruise on her thigh. I was called to see her, and this was a new problem with no family or past medical history of bleeding or bruising. There is a well-established panel of laboratory tests to check for abnormal bleeding, but these were all normal. And then an unlikely possibility dawned on me: could she have developed a very rare antibody which had neutralised and destroyed her coagulation factor XIII? This factor provides the final nuts and bolts locking together the fibres of a blood clot, and deficiency is so rare that it is not tested for in a routine blood coagulation screen. It was indeed completely absent in her blood, and without the treatment we rapidly started, she would have almost certainly died from a brain haemorrhage. The brief report was published in *The Lancet* and seemed to provoke much interest amongst my medical colleagues. However, rather like the rare patient I saw at the Marsden, they would very likely go several lifetimes without ever seeing a case.

Alice was a pretty girl with a triangular-shaped face and odd deformed thumbs. These features helped me make the diagnosis of Fanconi anaemia in her teens, which is unusual as most cases are recognised in infancy. This rare inherited condition is due to a defect in the complex systems which ordinarily repair background damage to DNA, and such patients have a high risk of developing leukaemia. With the agreement of Alice and her parents we sampled her bone marrow every six months and changes to her chromosomes came and went – genetic storms were raging in her marrow cells which were previously unseen. The idea was that if we could predict the final irreversible slide into leukaemia, a bone marrow transplant could be performed. "But why not do it anyway?" I hear you ask. Well, as you have heard, a transplant is a high-risk procedure and she may have remained fit and healthy for many years before the inevitable progression to leukaemia occurred. I was pleased to have a brief report accepted by an American journal, but more gratified when, a few years later, sequential genetic changes in the bone marrow of a large series of Fanconi patients was published by an American research group in the Premier League. I may be wrong, but I like to think that my modest case report from the Third Division encouraged this important study.

I may have shown courage when I put my hand up to volunteer to box in the school tournament all those years ago, but I was going to avoid this challenge if at all possible. The mere thought filled me with horror and my internal risk-assessment monitor was registering in the danger zone.

Towards the end of our training, it was thought useful for haematology trainees to have the experience of a short spell of technical on-call covering hospital laboratory duties out of hours. Routine laboratory work in haematology and other disciplines of pathology is normally performed by biomedical scientists. These are all highly trained graduates who work in close cooperation with medical staff. Amongst many other duties, they operate the highly sophisticated machines and instruments which generate blood counts, coagulation test results and complex data for the accurate diagnosis of leukaemias, including gene analysis and studies on DNA. The specialist knowledge of these colleagues is invaluable for interpreting the technical information produced by the laboratory. In addition, they have special skills in blood transfusion to ensure that safe, compatible blood products are provided for patients. Overnight, perhaps only one or two scientists would be at work in a major hospital covering all these activities, and this was the nerve-racking experience I was making every attempt to avoid. Quite simply, I knew my limitations and this was very specialist work requiring a skill set which I felt was beyond me. Life-and-death decisions in the clinic was one thing, but checking blood compatibility at a bench in the transfusion laboratory at 3am filled me with foreboding. You do remember my bench skills making suppositories and pastilles, I hope!

Sometimes our colleagues would be overwhelmed if multiple casualties appeared in the A&E department or a patient with a ruptured aortic aneurysm had to be taken to theatre. Vast amounts of blood and plasma had to be carefully checked and issued, and urgent results provided; the bleep and telephone constantly interrupting their concentration as they performed this important work. I remember my bleary-eyed colleague Ben telling me one morning that he had issued forty units of blood and numerous bags of plasma and platelets for a stabbing victim with a lacerated liver the previous night. I always had great respect for my laboratory colleagues and thought they were undervalued at times for the responsibility and the level of commitment they showed. And yes, I kept my head down and did avoid the nightmare scenario of trying to emulate their expertise and competence in the early hours.

I peered at the skull, blackened and deformed. It was human, but many of the features lacked familiarity and were unlike any that I remembered from medical school. Deep-set eye sockets, nasal cartilage missing but dentition intact. Odd motifs, and was it made of bone or metal? My wife and I were at a Grayson Perry exhibition and I was attempting to interpret the thoughts behind *Head of a Fallen Giant* before checking with his crib sheet.

I admire Mr Perry's art, and not just because he was born in Essex. He adds to the gaiety of life, and I like the raw humanity of the man and the fact that he doesn't feel the need to cloak his work in obscurity. He is happy to describe the thoughts and feelings which brought his art into existence, and is a great communicator. Looking at his wall hangings, I drifted to thoughts of a well-worn metaphor; the tapestry of life interwoven with different-coloured threads and unique stitches. How much would the picture differ if I hadn't been to university and medical school? I like to think that the essence of my character would have been little different, but some social skills have certainly been learnt. And the ability to communicate. Working in a hospital, the whole day is spent communicating with different groups: patients, nurses, students, laboratory staff, porters, fellow doctors; constantly switching hats according to the flavour of the interaction. A long way from my early years, when I stuttered self-consciously on the phone and turned pink when speaking in public. Only hospital management proved difficult to communicate with at times; the language of the MBA dealing with systems, processes and a steady flow of kneejerk paperwork. Knowing costs but not value, managers often lacked the vocabulary used by those with an overriding concern for individual patients.

As the years pass, it is often possible to recognise circles and patterns in the turn of events. Life can have a strange habit of providing unexpected surprises when past experiences are brought back into sharp focus. Recently I visited an elderly aunt in her nursing home. She is ninety-four years old and I am her power of attorney. As I surveyed the sitting room of elderly residents, my mind returned to the first patients I cared for in the geriatric ward at Harold Wood Hospital. The same cornucopia of human stories: love, loss, triumph and disappointment, pain and joy, drifting to a gentle conclusion. Sitting close by were two old chaps, also in their nineties, who were in the home for respite care, and I overheard them mention their wartime experiences. Engaging William in conversation, he told me that he had fought with the 6th Gurkha Rifles. On mentioning that my father had been a Royal Marine on HMS *Belfast*, his face and eyes lit up.

"Oh, they were tough boys!" he said, and I returned my father's admiration for the Gurkhas.

"Our Gurkha boys used to go down into the tunnels and flush the Japanese out with grenades," he said, with obvious pride and admiration. "And we used to shoot them as they came up the foxholes at the other end!"

Many would think that there are few positives in this tale, but do not be too quick to condemn. The Japanese ploy was to allow our troops to pass by and then spring from their lairs and shoot them in the back.

I thanked him for his bravery on my behalf, and as we parted, I heard him say to his friend, "That was nice, I don't hear much appreciation for our efforts these days."

One person who would have shown appreciation if he had been there was my old friend from medical school, Peter. He has a fascination with military history and visits scenes of famous battles. On one occasion, in the Highlands village of Braemar, we visited a tiny enclosure with a granite stone commemorating the war dead. He placed a small cross with a poppy taken from a hidden pocket with the words *Thanks, chaps* added in his own hand.

11

Ten Years After

It was 1989, ten years after my father's death, and I went to see my colleague Dr Bharat Jasani, a histopathologist, to determine whether he could help me with a research area I was studying at the time. As we chewed over the project, I noticed a reprint of a paper to the side of me on the bench. It was a publication on mesothelioma and, not surprisingly, I briefly sidetracked into the family saga.

Bharat looked thoughtful. "You do know that we have an international expert in the field over at Llandough Hospital the other side of the city?" he said. "Alan Gibbs."

"No," I replied. Our paths had not crossed even though I had worked at the hospital briefly.

"Why don't you have a word with him?" Bharat prompted.

And so I made my way over to Llandough and met Alan. He sat and listened to the unfolding story, becoming more intrigued as one surprising twist followed another.

"Well, I definitely think it is worth taking forward," he said after I had finished. "It was really important that you demanded a coroner's post-mortem when your father died; it means that somewhere we should be able to find the stored histological slides which have to be kept for thirty years. I will see what I can do."

I left Alan's office with mixed feelings. We had laid both my father and the asbestos saga to rest all those years ago – would it be right for me to stir up memories and emotions again after such a time? On the other hand, if the diagnosis was revisited and the cause of Dad's death was confirmed as asbestos-related, I could look him in the metaphysical eye and say that we had achieved truth and justice on his behalf. I decided to mark time and wait to see whether Alan had any success with his search.

Some weeks later, he contacted me. He had reviewed the slides and, yes, they did show mesothelioma. In fact, to a histopathologist and expert in the field, the diagnosis was obvious just on simple staining. As a bonus, however, special immunocytochemistry techniques showed that the material was positive for cytokeratin and negative for carcinoembryonic antigen; a pattern of staining strongly pointing to mesothelioma rather than carcinoma. The correct diagnosis was not in doubt. Even with the forewarning, this was still something of a shock. As a family, we had buried our suspicions deep as we became grudgingly reconciled to the miscarriage of justice.

The moral dilemma persisted, but there seemed little choice but to tell my mother that the coda to our journey could be rewritten if she so wished. In fact, she took the news more calmly than I anticipated and her feelings were dominated by relief and righteousness.

Would she have the strength to open old emotional wounds and take the case further, if necessary fighting for legal recognition that the death had resulted from an industrial disease? She thought she could, based on the second-hand experiences of my two aunts who previously fought for compensation from Turner & Newall. In the case of Dave, it had taken his widow, Else, eight and a half years to receive payment from the company. Even where the diagnosis was unequivocal from the beginning, every means was used by the firm's legal team to prevaricate and throw up obstacles to slow the pursuit of justice.

The first step was to contact the Post Office Union which, after a short deliberation, confirmed that it would cover the costs of the case and support an action against Turner & Newall on my mother's behalf. When he was alive, the union helped my father fight for a living wage to support an ailing wife and bring up three children. After his death, it was a critical ally in our fight to bring him justice. A barrister with specialist knowledge of asbestos claims was appointed from a London Chambers. One of the first pieces of advice from the legal team was that, despite strong circumstantial evidence, we should try to secure clear documentation that George actually worked with asbestos when he was employed by the company in the late 1930s. This would come from his war records – there, plain as day on his enlistment papers, was his occupation: *asbestos boiler coverer*. Behind the scenes I continued to work with the union and our legal team for the next year or two.

Asbestos has been used by man for over four thousand years, and Pliny the Elder commented on the sickness of slaves who mined the material in the first century AD. It is a group of six types of silicate mineral composed of fine, fibrous crystals, each containing millions of microscopic fibrils. They are recognised by their colours – blue, white and brown – which have different uses. Unique properties including resistance to heat, fire and electricity led to its widespread application for building insulation and for pipe and boiler lagging, and the manufacture of brake pads, shoes and fire safety equipment. The mineral can also be mixed with plaster and cement to produce asbestos sheeting for construction. Turner & Newall was later to pioneer a product called 'Limpet', which was sprayed onto surfaces as fire protection and for soundproofing. In the past, it has even found use in dental-cast linings and cigarette filters, as if tobacco wasn't carcinogenic enough! Although asbestos mining and industrial application have declined significantly in the developed world, production and widespread use of the mineral have continued in the developing world including Brazil, Russia, China and India. All the different types are dangerous to health and can induce chronic lung fibrosis (asbestosis) as well as mesothelioma and lung cancer.

In patients like my father and uncles exposed to asbestos, microscopic examination of their lungs often shows asbestos bodies; fibres which cannot be eliminated by scavenger cells in the tissue and persist long term. Individual crystals are coated with an iron-rich protein which helps them to be identified in the sections. Mesothelioma is a malignancy of the mesothelial cells which line the inner surface of the thoracic and abdominal cavities. The cancer is specifically associated with asbestos exposure, and the microscopic appearance shows many variant forms. Some have superficial resemblance to more common carcinomas, but an expert can generally discriminate between the two, and the additional techniques employed by Alan Gibbs are important in the more difficult cases.

Turner & Newall was one of the biggest players in the asbestos game. Founded in Rochdale in 1871 as Turner Brothers, the company changed its name to Turner Brothers Asbestos Company in 1879. Later in 1920 it would merge with Newall Insulation Company, and was listed on the Stock Exchange. Other asbestos companies were absorbed in the US and UK, and asbestos mines were developed and operated in Southern Africa. In the 1930s and '40s extensive mining interests were also acquired in Canada and factories manufacturing asbestos products were opened throughout the UK including in Widnes, Tamworth, Glasgow and South Wales. The company enjoyed over 60% of the massive asbestos market, had a thirty-six-thousand-strong workforce, and the commercial value of the product was acknowledged by naming its headquarters Asbestos House. As the health risks of the mineral became apparent in the 1970s and '80s, however, the demand for asbestos products declined rapidly and it was banned from all use in the UK in 1999. Some commentators have raised concerns, however, that imminent changes to our trading arrangements with the United States could again see products containing the mineral enter the country. American environmental agencies still allow asbestos to be incorporated into a number of products including roofing materials and brake linings.

The company had the opportunity to accept its liability and guilt and settle out of court. Instead, to our surprise, it chose to defend the case at the High Court in London. Surprise because it accepted that George had worked for the company and that the diagnosis of mesothelioma was secure. Furthermore, the company conceded that *by virtue of [their] negligent exposure of the deceased to asbestos dust he contracted the malignancy.* Instead, the company's argument against culpability was that the *actual* cause of death – myocardial infarction due to coronary thrombosis – was unrelated to the mesothelioma and therefore not due to asbestos exposure. Bringing an expensive case to court on such tenuous and frankly spurious grounds still seems very odd to me. Any medically qualified person would know that this was nonsense. Cancers can be the primary cause of death if, for example, the patient gradually declines and wastes away with advanced cachexia; the body simply giving up the fight in the terminal stages. Sometimes, a tumour will erode into a blood vessel and death will result from massive bleeding. Much more commonly, however, the physiological and biochemical changes induced by an advanced cancer predispose the patient to thrombosis as a terminal event, usually via a blood clot in the lung, but sometimes in an artery to cause a stroke or coronary thrombosis. Infection might supervene in other patients and bring a welcome relief by ending the process of decline, or the electrolyte abnormalities in the blood could lead to a fatal cardiac arrhythmia. To argue that such events and the underlying malignancy are not linked is clearly ridiculous. In fact, a paper in the journal *Cancer* was published contemporaneously with the case coming to court which confirmed that, over the two years prior to presentation with malignancy, patients have a markedly increased risk of ischaemic heart disease and myocardial infarction, and that the risk is even higher in those with disseminated disease.

Unfortunately, this did not come to the attention of our counsel or myself; otherwise the case might have been open and shut.

Perhaps the company was concerned that our retrospective diagnosis, which must have had no precedent, posed a particular threat and could open a floodgate of similar claims in the future. It was therefore willing to fight the case on the off chance that it might win on the medical technicality. Did Turner & Newall think it was taking the battle to a little grey-haired lady susceptible to bullying and not realise that there was a highly qualified academic and physician standing just behind her? Or perhaps it was related in some obscure way to another major and far-reaching threat the company was under at the time? Hiding behind weak Freedom of Information rules in the UK, Turner & Newall had always maintained an arrogant pose of denial and obfuscation when records or company correspondence were requested by opposing legal teams. However, although it was undoubtedly a large shark on this side of the corporate ocean, an orca in the form of a major US bank was circling menacingly and would strike without mercy. The British company had been responsible for providing and fitting insulation material containing asbestos in the Chase Manhattan Bank in New York. When the bank decided to sell the real estate, they found that the market value had been greatly reduced and they sought damages of $180 million to cover the cost of the mineral's safe removal. The bank needed to demonstrate that Turner & Newall knew about the health risks of asbestos beforehand and, using powerful Freedom of Information statutes in America, they forced the British company to disclose hundreds of thousands of historical documents from their hitherto unknown vaults in Manchester. This disclosure would, in fact, be the future death knell for the company. The evidence could not be denied; the documents confirmed that Turner & Newall was aware of the serious health concerns very early in the twentieth century and recognised the risk this posed to the profitability of the company. The correspondence laid bare all the nefarious means used by the company to avoid culpability.

Michael O'Connor, the vice president of Chase Manhattan Bank, went a step further. He released the documents and made them freely available to all the attorneys and British legal teams fighting for asbestos victims in the courts both in America and the UK. He was to receive a Freedom of Information Award from the Labour leader Tony Blair in 1995 for this selfless action.

And so it came to the week when the case was due to be heard at the High Court of Justice in the Strand. My mother, sister and I travelled up each day and entered through a revolving side door rather than the huge portal so familiar from news clips of important criminal appeals. Judge Mitchell gave a brief address summarising the basis of the case in legal technicalities before our barrister, Mr Kieran May, and the opposing counsel laid out the arguments of the two sides which would be addressed with the support of witnesses. We were called to the stand first. I felt comfortable answering questions from the opposing counsel, assured by the righteousness of our cause and familiar with formal public speaking and lecturing. But I was proud of my mother. Small and vulnerable, she sat in the witness box and looked fragile in the intimidating surroundings. However, she was determined not to be daunted by this new challenge. After all, by her twenties she had lost both parents, fought her way out of East End poverty, negotiated a World War and confronted a near-fatal illness. Speaking clearly and slowly as I had instructed, she kept her emotions in check and gave a convincing and authentic story of what she knew of George's occupational history, the family saga, and her personal recollections of the last days of his illness. Alan Gibbs received quite a grilling on the technical aspects of the cause of death, but did not waver from the obvious truth that it resulted from mesothelioma even though the pathological events occurring in the blood vessels of the heart in the final hours were the last link in the chain. Kieran May then called a forceful consultant in lung diseases, Dr Robin Rudd from the London Chest Hospital, who bulldozed through the arguments of the defence counsel in a confident and mildly disdainful manner.

I was pleased he was on our side. He took no prisoners and I suspect that this was not the first time he had crossed swords with the facing adversaries.

I'm rather hazy now about the witnesses called by the opposing counsel – apart from one. Dr Dewi Davis was an old teacher of mine who was a consultant physician in Nottingham. He was a delightful man; an old-fashioned tuberculosis specialist who, towards the end of his career, had unexpectedly been caught up in the wind of change which was the opening of the new medical school. At that time I had much to learn from this experienced senior physician. We exchanged some small talk in the anteroom and, whether because of our previous association or his lack of true conviction in the veracity of their case, he gave a rather diffident and unconvincing performance on the stand.

Fortunately, I have little experience of courts or the legal system. I have to say, though, that I was very impressed by Judge Mitchell, who presided over the case. Perceptive and with surgical precision, his occasional utterances showed that he was always up to speed with the arguments even when quite complex medical matters were being discussed,

"I am minded to discount that argument on the grounds that..." was commonly heard, or, "I hear what you say, but..." which meant that he was not going to be fooled or misled by devious means. At times the opposing counsels would squabble like children and he would call them to order with a parent's firm command. The opposing teams had no doubt who was in charge of the proceedings.

On the fifth day it was time to hear Judge Mitchell's deliberations on the case and his final verdict. The arguments were summarised in unbiased fashion before the conclusion was delivered – in our favour. Relief, elation, a sense of order and closure. A myriad of emotions as my mother whispered a simple, stifled "Yes" in response. The judge set damages at £85,000 plus costs, but I can honestly say that this was of subsidiary importance. As my mother said, "How can you put a price on a long and happy marriage, you can't can you?" We left by the imposing main door and were met by a barrage of press and cameras as my mother and our legal team gave brief comment. And then home to a cup of tea, quiet reflections on what we had achieved and, we hoped, a slow return to normality.

Though warned by our legal representatives that there would be a good deal of press interest in the case, we were unprepared for the very wide coverage it received. That evening after the judgement, both London Weekend Television and BBC South East led with the story as part of major segments on the rising mesothelioma epidemic and the culpability of Turner & Newall. It was an odd feeling seeing my parents' wedding photographs on the screen, and also a rare picture showing the three brothers with my grandfather and grandmother. There I was in the centre, a baby cradled in Nanny Alice's lap. We recorded the news items on video and I recently transferred them to DVD. My mother gave brief comments on her mixed feelings and my brother, sister and I, though much younger than now, have serious and worn faces from the stressful days in court. Kieran May was interviewed and highlighted the importance to the outcome of the documents seized by the attorneys of the Chase Manhattan Bank, saying, "It made all the difference." The key piece of information amongst the numerous damning company reports and correspondence was that Turner & Newall were well aware of the risk of mesothelioma associated with asbestos products by 1932. He speculated that the documents would open the floodgates for future claims, and this prediction proved correct.

The case was top of the news agenda for a week or more, with a large spread and photographs in the *Daily Mail* and articles in the *Romford Times* and *Bristol Evening Post*. Then in 1994, the BBC broadcast an edition of *Taking Liberties*, presented by the investigative reporter John Ware, which was entitled *An Acceptable Level of Death*.

The programme summarised all the evidence against Turner & Newall and highlighted a series of bereaved families, including my mother and two aunts. Viewed twenty-five years later, it is a very moving experience to hear these three women describe the final days of their much-loved husbands, and it reminds me how relatively young they were when their lives were destroyed. Kieran May again took part and described a strategy he used in our case which I was unaware of. He wrote to the company board beforehand and asked them explicitly whether they had documents relating to my father's employment – when he already knew that this information had been found in America. The board replied in writing with an unequivocal denial, and their fate was sealed.

Turner & Newall brought a complaint against the programme to the Broadcasting Complaints Commission with a number of accusations of misrepresentation, but these were dismissed. It is difficult not to conclude that the documentary, together with the rest of the wide coverage of our case, was a significant factor in the final demise of this multinational company. Facing an overwhelming number of asbestos-related lawsuits, Turner & Newall filed for Chapter 11 bankruptcy in 2001.

At the end of John Ware's programme he attempted to interview the chairman of Turner & Newall at a posh London reception for the great and the good. There was the odd politician in the background looking smug and self-satisfied. The chairman was challenged on behalf of the small and insignificant people dying as a result of the company's exploitation.

Why was false information provided by his company in the UK when it conflicted with the true facts revealed by their documents in the States, the reporter enquired?

Dressed in a penguin suit and carrying a cane, he responded with anger and pompous disdain at the effrontery of Mr Ware to approach him on such matters. As I looked at his face contorted in contempt, I thought of Ayn Rand, the populist and libertarian philosopher of the 1940s. In her fourth novel, *Atlas Shrugged*, she promotes the idea of rampant capitalism unfettered by regulation or statutory constraint. It was a clarion call against unionised labour, fair taxation and any government intervention which diverted resources away from the elite and towards the disadvantaged. Only industrialists, business leaders and intellectual thinkers like herself had value in a world where there was "no such thing as society". Lacking humanity and compassion, the chairman would have fitted in so well as a character in Rand's novel. His obituary in 2015 tells us that *he served on a panel of industrial advisors to John Major and was knighted in 1996.*

A number of well-researched books and academic articles have been published over the years on the historical misdemeanours of asbestos companies. All the predictable consequences are highlighted when commerce and industry fail to be subjected to close governmental oversight and scrutiny. Elastic morality applied to company values, a duty of care to the bottom line rather than workers' rights and safety, and undue consideration given to the 'needy' demands of shareholders. Powerful critics of the industry were silenced or deflected with inducements and their influence subverted by political pressure. The texts describe how well-funded legal teams used every means possible to parry criticism and use technicalities and shady interpretations to delay justice for victims. And how the fundamental processes of scientific enquiry were corrupted by generous support for industry-backed conventions; guest speakers primed to support their cause and 'fake news' pseudoscientific papers published in journals of questionable merit and standing. Full use was made of weak or absent trade unions and malleable local politicians in countries where asbestos was mined. When politicians periodically call for a bonfire of regulations and red tape constraining the animal spirits of free enterprise, be careful to interrogate their true motives and what you allow them to enact. As the old adage goes, and my wife constantly reminds me, the lessons of history have to be constantly revisited.

Addendum:

I really don't think the building industry understands how fire behaves in buildings and how dangerous it can be. The government's mania for deregulation means our current safety standards just aren't good enough. (Architect and fire expert Sam Webb, commenting on the Grenfell Tower fire and quoted in the Guardian, 14th June 2017.)

12

If Atlas Shrugs

Sitting in the court as a qualified cancer specialist seeking belated justice for my father, the two great sagas of my life seem to merge and coalesce. When we sat in the park in virtual silence all those years ago, a few months before his death and my final examinations, he knew he was dying and he knew the cause. And I believe he did know I would do the right thing and ensure that the truth would be told and that my mother would receive recompense for her pain and loss, both in terms of justice and financial security in the future. So I did carry a well-hidden sense that I owed him a debt until the deed was done. My mother would not have lived in poverty if the claim had not been brought but, as a woman of simple needs, the financial compensation ensured that she wanted for nothing in her final years.

I regret not having a candid conversation with my father about his illness when I had the opportunity. In the modern era and in Western culture, a patient with a terminal condition is generally informed of their prognosis by their doctor. Bioethicists advise that individual autonomy and self-determination are the paramount principles, and the days of medical paternalism are long gone. Openness allows plans for a 'good death' to be formulated in partnership with relatives and carers and the patient can be given time to get their affairs in order – most obviously financial, but also in terms of wider relationships and possibly the spiritual sphere. A sense of isolation can be avoided. I'm sure that a quiet, confidential word enabling me to share Dad's secret world would have strengthened the bond between father and son in the last few months of his life. Of course, this is all with the hindsight of my many years' experience dealing, I hope sympathetically, with dying patients and their families.

Trust is the key component in these sensitive areas of communication, but unfortunately this abstract noun seems to have passed its sell-by-date in recent times. Politicians cannot be trusted to be motivated by the common good, professional groups cannot be trusted to avoid favouring their vested interests; the police, teachers, the media; everyone under constant scrutiny, with suspicion the default position. Though under threat from the internet and tabloid paranoia, perhaps the NHS doctor-patient relationship is one of the last vestiges of trust in our society. The patient must know that everything the doctor recommends and advises is in their best interests. As the old adage goes, they must trust that the physician will advise and treat them as they would their own loved ones. Dealing with the fear, anxiety and existential uncertainty of patients in a supportive partnership has been the most fundamental privilege and satisfaction of being a doctor. The unique appeal and challenge of the role is that every day one has to deal, face-to-face and in a practical way, with the complexity and mystery of the human condition.

Not long ago, at home, I heard a stuttering belly laugh as my six-year-old grandson appeared. I knew that sound, a musical trait sounding through the generations. And did that voice have just a trace of resemblance to the recording of the young son welcoming his father on the quayside all those years ago? I had called him from his play to show him his ancestors. He fixed me with brown eyes and, although George's genes might not be entirely responsible, those dark pools reminded me of him. I recently collected all my parents' old photographs and scanned them into a photobook. Lin also found pictures of my great-grandparents and other long-lost treasures on the internet, which I included. In this way, I have tried to freeze those moments and memories of my parents and ancestors for posterity. My father's bravery in war, respected character in the workplace and courage in his terminal illness are shining signposts which have directed my own life, although, as I have previously said, he was a hard act to follow. Hopefully I have given the next generation a perception of the man which they can draw on to guide their own progress through life.

My mother died at the age of eighty-six, a remarkable feat given the number of Damocles swords which pierced the ground around her in those early years. She fought all the way during her final journey, just as she did against all the other adversities in her life. Only Dorothy now survives from that generation of Daltreys to check and confirm my half-remembered truths. She finds distant memories easiest to recall now, and though we laugh as we reminisce, she admits that those times were very often far from the 'good old days'.

Throughout this book I have described a series of meaningful coincidences, and not least the fellowship of tragedy on HMS *Dunedin* which led to my birth. Finding some old chemistry books on a market stall, meeting my wife in the last week of the last term at university, and spotting a reprint on Bharat Jasani's bench – each setting off a train of events which could have barely been anticipated but in retrospect had a sense of the inevitable.

On a lighter note, and as a football fan, our return to Nottingham coinciding with the appointment of Brian Clough at the City Ground might be another. When my parents visited our first house, I took my father to see an undistinguished goalless draw with West Bromwich Albion, but I was pleased that we spent the precious time together. My friend Peter and I went to many Forest games when they were on the brink of greatness, and we watched Woodcock, Withe and Robertson weave such intricate patterns with such speed and skill that there was no surprise at the club's future success. Irresistible in his self-belief, the redoubtable and unpredictable Mr Clough took a disparate group of journeymen, novice youngsters and late bloomers and fashioned a team capable of winning two European Cups; the humble beginnings and added value enhancing the satisfaction of the achievement.

There must be many people who would see my story purely as a triumph of personal effort over circumstances. That social advancement and academic success can be achieved by anyone from a humble background with a combination of hard work and delayed gratification. In my view, however, good fortune played a large part in any modest accomplishments I have achieved. There is also little doubt that generous support from both individuals and institutions has been vital along the way – if there was any truth in the notion that "There is no such thing as society", I would not be writing this now. Help from dedicated teachers prepared to invest in lost causes, lecturers going the extra mile, modest but critical funding from central government and local authorities and, in particular, the NHS for saving my mother's life and restoring some normality to a chaotic early childhood. And, of course, being blessed with a wife who put my hopes, dreams and aspirations before her own. The world has undoubtedly changed since the days of my childhood and most would agree that the contemporary moral code is 'winner takes all'. There has been a steady shift in society towards the cult of individuality and away from collective responsibility for the common good. Would it still be possible for a present-day poor, displaced ragamuffin wandering Tilbury Marshes to aspire to become a doctor? If Atlas shrugs, could that youngster rely on the selfish and self-centred to help him achieve his dream?

And so I return to our journey for a final time. Life moved on and, at the age of nearly forty, I struggled through the last set of exams to become a Member of the Royal College of Pathologists. The door to a consultant post was open and a new life beckoned. We paused briefly to enjoy a moment in the sunshine with the breeze on our faces before my wife and I, ever the loving partnership, went forward together to begin writing the next chapter.

As the famous philosopher once wrote, *There may be more beautiful times but this one is ours.*